Your True Home

Your True Home

The Everyday Wisdom of Thich Nhat Hanh

Compiled and edited
BY MELVIN MCLEOD

SHAMBHALA
Boulder | 2011

SHAMBHALA PUBLICATIONS, INC.
2129 13th Street
Boulder, Colorado 80302
www.shambhala.com

©2011 by Unified Buddhist Church, Inc. Published by arrangement with the
Unified Buddhist Church, Inc., 2496 Melru Lane, Escondido, CA 92026 USA.

17 16 15 14 13 12 11

Printed in the United States of America

Shambhala Publications makes every effort to print on acid-free, recycled
paper.

Shambhala Publications is distributed worldwide by Penguin Random House,
Inc., and its subsidiaries.

Library of Congress Cataloging-in-Publication Data
Nhât Hạnh, Thích.
[Selections. 2011]
Your true home: the everyday wisdom of Thich Nhat Hanh /
by Thich Nhat Hanh; compiled and edited by Melvin McLeod.—1st ed.
p.   cm.
Includes bibliographical references and index.
ISBN 978-1-59030-926-1 (pbk.)
1. Nhât Hạnh, Thích—Quotations. I. McLeod, Melvin. II. Title.
BQ9800.T5392N452 2011
294.3'4432—dc22
2011014497

CONTENTS

EDITOR'S PREFACE

THIS BOOK OFFERS us a precious gift. It is an offering of insight—of deep and relevant truths—from one of the great spiritual teachers of our time.

Insight is a mysterious, almost miraculous experience. A flash of insight can come upon us in a moment, without warning, like the opening in a cloudy sky that suddenly illuminates the landscape below. We see simply and clearly what before had been hidden in the shadows of concepts and confusion. This direct and immediate experience of reality, so surprising and yet somehow so familiar, can transform our life.

We may not know when or even why such moments of insight will occur, but there are ways we can make them more likely. One is contemplating the wisdom of a great spiritual teacher like Thich Nhat Hanh. His role as a Buddhist master is to transmit to us the insight he has gained in a long life of study and meditation. In the Buddhist tradition, that transmission can take place over the course of years—or in a moment. A phrase, a single word, a blow, or a shout can be enough to wake us up. Or a paragraph or two of profound truth and instruction—like those on every page of this book.

Of course the spiritual teacher can only offer us his or her wisdom; it is up to us to be ready to accept it. So how you read this book will make all the difference in how these teachings affect and benefit you.

We may think that true insight is complex and requires many words to explain, but the reverse is closer to the truth: the simple statements are often the most profound. It would be easy to surround the short teachings in this book with lots of supporting arguments and illustrations. But they've been pared away, and what we're left with are some of Buddhism's—and life's—essential truths as taught by one of the most important Buddhist masters of our time. These are not mere aphorisms to cheer us up or inspire us (although they do both). They are transformative insights and instructions, and we need to let them seep below the surface level of our intellect into our heart and guts, where wisdom gestates and real change happens.

Take the concept of impermanence. If we look at it purely from the level of intellect—give it a quick read and move on—it seems obvious and perhaps not very meaningful. But impermanence is actually the central tenet of Buddhism, because its denial is the source of our suffering. If we actually contemplate the reality of impermanence, if we reach the point where we really see ourselves and our world as ever changing, interdependent, and without fixed identity, then our life, as Thich Nhat Hanh tells us, changes dramatically. It becomes joyous, loving, and magical.

Take another central teaching of this book: living in the present, without losing ourselves in thoughts of the past or future. Looked at superficially, that could be just another New Age bromide. But truly practiced, it's the essence of Buddhist meditation and the path back to our true home, as Thich Nhat Hanh calls the present moment.

Perhaps it is the very simplicity of these teachings that makes them so difficult for us to realize. We believe that real truth must be complicated and far away, so we don't see what's right in front of us.

That's why we have to lay the ground properly for those precious moments of insight to happen. That's why we shouldn't read this book so much as contemplate and practice it. When I read one of the short quotes in this book, I feel as if I am sitting right in front of this great master, hearing him personally offer his most important teachings. If you choose to read this book that way, you can have the same experience. It will multiply the benefit many times.

I urge you to read these teachings slowly and carefully, one or two a day maybe, savoring and contemplating their deeper meaning. I have found that the teachings I read in the morning seep into my consciousness and haunt my day. Their wisdom subtly colors my experience, and insights and reminders arise as if on their own, yet always at an appropriate moment. Please give these great teachings the space and time to haunt you too.

The pithy teachings in this book fall into two broad categories: insight and instruction. Some offer clear, direct insights into the nature of reality. They reveal the true nature of phenomena, the mind, neurosis, suffering, and enlightenment. They cover topics as deep and diverse as interbeing, emptiness, aimlessness, Buddhahood, and nirvana. They epitomize Buddhist wisdom.

Others offer instruction on a wide range of meditation practices, from mindfulness and insight to loving-kindness and compassion. They guide us in the formal practices of mindful sitting, breathing, and walking, and in all the ways we can bring the mind of meditation into our daily lives, from improving our relationships and healing our emotional wounds, to promoting peace in the world and protecting our environment. It is meditation that develops insight, and insight that changes our life and our world for the better. It is all here.

The variety and depth of these teachings reflect the extraordinary life of this Buddhist master. He wanted to be a monk from a very young age, and entered a Zen monastery in his native Vietnam at sixteen. He combined intense meditation practice and study with the fiery spirit of a reformer, and quickly became a progressive force within Vietnamese Buddhism and an important leader of the Engaged Buddhist movement working for peace and social justice in Vietnam. A courageous antiwar activist who earned the enmity of both sides in the Vietnam War with his impartial campaign for peace, he was nominated for the Nobel Peace Prize by Martin Luther King, Jr. In 1967, he was exiled from Vietnam and not allowed to return to his native land for thirty-nine years.

Today, Thich Nhat Hanh has tens of thousands of students worldwide, and millions have benefited from the more than seventy books he has written, which range from scholarly texts and meditation handbooks to psychology, children's books, and commentary on the important social and political questions of our times. Zen master, statesman, humanitarian, poet, and leader of the Engaged Buddhist movement, Thich Nhat Hanh brings his wisdom and skill to the full range of human experience as no other spiritual teacher today does.

It has been a great honor for me to edit this collection, for which I thank my friends at Shambhala Publications, and above all, the great teacher Thich Nhat Hanh. These jewels of wisdom and insight have changed my life, as they may yours. They are enough for a year. They are enough for a lifetime.

> MELVIN MCLEOD
> Editor in chief
> *The Shambhala Sun*
> *Buddhadharma: The Practitioner's Quarterly*
> *Mindful: Living with Awareness and Compassion*

Your True Home

I

Your True Home

YOUR TRUE HOME is in the here and the now. It is not limited by time, space, nationality, or race. Your true home is not an abstract idea; it is something you can touch and live in every moment. With mindfulness and concentration, the energies of the Buddha, you can find your true home in the full relaxation of your mind and body in the present moment.

2

One Hundred Percent

BE THERE TRULY. Be there with 100 percent of yourself. In every moment of your daily life. That is the essence of true Buddhist meditation. Each of us knows that we can do that, so let us train to live each moment of our daily life deeply. That is why I like to define *mindfulness* as the energy that helps us to be there 100 percent. It is the energy of your true presence.

———

3
Miracles

AROUND US, LIFE bursts forth with miracles—a glass of water, a ray of sunshine, a leaf, a caterpillar, a flower, laughter, raindrops. If you live in awareness, it is easy to see miracles everywhere. Each human being is a multiplicity of miracles. Eyes that see thousands of colors, shapes, and forms; ears that hear a bee flying or a thunderclap; a brain that ponders a speck of dust as easily as the entire cosmos; a heart that beats in rhythm with the heartbeat of all beings. When we are tired and feel discouraged by life's daily struggles, we may not notice these miracles, but they are always there.

4

Ambassador of the Cosmos

WHEN I HOLD A piece of bread, I look at it, and sometimes I smile at it. The piece of bread is an ambassador of the cosmos offering nourishment and support. Looking deeply into the piece of bread, I see the sunshine, the clouds, the great earth. Without the sunshine, no wheat can grow. Without the clouds, there is no rain for the wheat to grow. Without the great earth, nothing can grow. That is why the piece of bread that I hold in my hand is a wonder of life. It is there for all of us. We have to be there for it.

5

Walking Meditation

WE HAVE TO AWAKEN ourselves to the truth that we are here, alive. We are here making steps on this beautiful planet. This is already performing a miracle. But we have to be here in order for the miracle to be possible. We have to bring ourselves back to the here and the now. Therefore, each step we take becomes a miracle. If you are able to walk like that, each step will be very nourishing and healing. You walk as if you kiss the earth with your feet, as if you massage the earth with your feet. There is a lot of love in that practice of walking meditation.

6

Concentration

WHEN YOU CONTEMPLATE the big, full sunrise, the more mindful and concentrated you are, the more the beauty of the sunrise is revealed to you. Suppose you are offered a cup of tea, very fragrant, very good tea. If your mind is distracted, you cannot really enjoy the tea. You have to be mindful of the tea, you have to be concentrated on it, so the tea can reveal its fragrance and wonder to you. That is why mindfulness and concentration are such sources of happiness. That's why a good practitioner knows how to create a moment of joy, a feeling of happiness, at any time of the day.

7
Why We Suffer

WHEN WE LOOK deeply at the nature of things, we see that in fact everything is impermanent. Nothing exists as a permanent entity; everything changes. It is said that we cannot step into the same river twice. If we look for a single, permanent entity in a river, we will not find it. The same is true of our physical body. There is no such thing as a self, no absolute, permanent entity to be found in the element we call "body." In our ignorance we believe that there is a permanent entity in us, and our pain and suffering manifest on the basis of that ignorance. If we touch deeply the nonself nature in us, we can get out of that suffering.

———

8

Suchness

THE WORD *suchness* describes reality as it is. Concepts and ideas are incapable of expressing reality as it is. Nirvana, the ultimate reality, cannot be described, because it is free of all concepts and ideas. Nirvana is the extinction of all concepts.

Most of our suffering arises from our ideas and concepts. If you are able to free yourself from these concepts, anxiety and fear will disappear. Nirvana, the ultimate reality, or God, is of the nature of no-birth and no-death. It is total freedom.

9

I Have Arrived

WE BELIEVE THAT happiness is possible only in the future. That is why the practice "I have arrived" is very important. The realization that we have already arrived, that we don't have to travel any further, that we are already here, can give us peace and joy. The conditions for our happiness are already sufficient. We only need to allow ourselves to be in the present moment, and we will be able to touch them.

10

Lotus in the Mud

THE GOODNESS OF suffering is something real. Without suffering there cannot be happiness. Without mud there cannot be any lotus flowers. So if you know *how* to suffer, suffering is OK. And the moment you have that attitude, you don't suffer much anymore. And out of suffering, a lotus flower of happiness can open.

11

Aimlessness

THERE IS A Buddhist teaching that might seem strange to you. This is the teaching of aimlessness (*apranihita* in Sanskrit). Aimlessness means not setting an object or goal in front of you and running after it. That is exactly what everybody does. We want this, we want that, and as long as we haven't got it, we think happiness will be impossible.

We must bring about a revolution in our thinking: we must stop. We must do as the flower does. The flower is aware of the fact that it contains everything within it, the whole cosmos, and it does not try to become something else. It is the same for you. You have God within you, so you do not have to look for God.

12

The Wave and the Water

THERE ARE TWO dimensions to life, and we should be able to touch both. One is like a wave, and we call it the "historical dimension." The other is like the water, and we call it the "ultimate dimension," or "nirvana." We usually touch just the wave, but when we discover how to touch the water, we receive the highest fruit that meditation can offer.

———

13
Freedom from Fear

BODHISATTVAS DWELL on the same ground as the rest of us—the world of birth and death, permanence, and self. But thanks to the practice of looking deeply into impermanence and nonself, they are in touch with the ultimate dimension, free from the fears associated with ideas of existence and nonexistence, one and many, coming and going, birth and death. In this freedom, they ride the waves of birth and death in perfect peace. They are able to remain in the world of waves while abiding in the nature of water.

14

I Am Here for You

THE HEART OF Buddhist practice is to generate our own presence in such a way that we can touch deeply the life that is here and available in every moment. We have to be here for ourselves; we have to be here for the people we love; we have to be here for life with all its wonders. The message of our Buddhist practice is simple and clear: "I am here for you."

15

The Foundation of Love

IF WE DO NOT know how to take care of ourselves and to love ourselves, we cannot take care of the people we love. Loving oneself is the foundation for loving another person.

————————

16

Embrace Them with Great Tenderness

DO NOT FIGHT against pain; do not fight against irritation or jealousy. Embrace them with great tenderness, as though you were embracing a little baby. Your anger is yourself, and you should not be violent toward it. The same thing goes for all of your emotions.

17

Becoming a Bodhisattva

IF WE MAKE a sincere effort to practice alleviating our inner suffering and the suffering of others, we too become bodhisattvas, awakened beings. We support our family, friends, and coworkers, and help them to manifest as bodhisattvas; we do this for the entire world and for the happiness of all beings. If through your practice you become a bodhisattva, those around you will see that beauty, genuine spirituality, and true love are possible. Living like this, you are happy and will become an inspiration for others.

18

The Next Buddha

TWO THOUSAND six hundred years ago, Shakyamuni Buddha proclaimed that the next Buddha will be named Maitreya, the "Buddha of Love." I think Maitreya Buddha may be a community, and not just an individual. A good community is needed to help us resist the unwholesome ways of our time. Mindful living protects us and helps us go in the direction of peace. With the support of friends in the practice, peace has a chance.

19

Flowers and Garbage

FLOWERS AND GARBAGE are both organic in nature. So looking deeply into the nature of a flower, you can see the presence of the compost and the garbage. The flower is also going to turn into garbage, but don't be afraid! You are a gardener, and you have in your hands the power to transform garbage into flowers, into fruit, into vegetables. You don't throw anything away, because you are not afraid of garbage. Your hands are capable of transforming it into flowers, or lettuce, or cucumbers.

The same thing is true of your happiness and your sorrow. Sorrow, fear, and depression are all a kind of garbage. These bits of garbage are part of real life, and we must look deeply into their nature. You can practice in order to turn these bits of garbage into flowers. It is not only your love that is organic; your hate is, too. So you should not throw anything out. All you have to do is learn how to transform your garbage into flowers.

20

A Visit from a Friend

SUPPOSE A FRIEND who has come a long way to visit is having a cup of tea with us. Mindfulness helps the time we spend with her to be a time we won't forget. We're not thinking of anything. We're not thinking of our business, our projects. We just focus our attention on this moment when we're with our friend. We're fully aware that she is there and that we can sit with her and enjoy a cup of tea. Mindfulness helps us to taste the joy of each moment very deeply.

———————

21

Life Is Not a Means to an End

WITH MINDFUL WALKING, our steps are no longer a means to arrive at an end. When we walk to the kitchen to serve our meal, we don't need to think, "I have to walk to the kitchen to get the food." With mindfulness, we can say, "I am enjoying walking to the kitchen," and each step is an end in itself. There is no distinction between means and ends. There is no way to happiness; happiness *is* the way. There is no way to enlightenment; enlightenment *is* the way.

———————

22

The Lamp of Mindfulness

WE HAVE A LAMP inside us, the lamp of mindfulness, which we can light anytime. The oil of that lamp is our breathing, our steps, and our peaceful smile. We have to light up that lamp of mindfulness so the light will shine out and the darkness will dissipate and cease. Our practice is to light up the lamp.

23

The Suffering of Those We Love

IF WE CAN HOLD OUR ANGER, our sorrow, and our fear with the energy of mindfulness, we will be able to recognize the roots of our suffering. We will be able to recognize the suffering in the people we love as well. Mindfulness helps us to not be angry at our loved ones, because when we are mindful, we understand that our loved ones are suffering as well.

———————

24

A Love Letter

IT'S THE ENERGY of mindfulness in us that allows us to write a real love letter and reconcile with another person. A real love letter is made of insight, understanding, and compassion. Otherwise it's not a love letter. A true love letter can produce a transformation in the other person, and therefore in the world. But before it produces a transformation in the other person, it has to produce a transformation within us. Some letters may take the whole of our lifetime to write.

———————

25

Selective Watering

THROUGH THE practice of deep looking, we can iden-
tify the positive seeds that we want to water every day,
and train ourselves not to water the negative ones. This
is called "selective watering." The Buddha recommended
methods for doing this, and even a few days of this practice can bring about a transformation.

———————

26

Sovereign of the Five Elements

EACH ONE OF US is sovereign over the territory of our own being and the five elements (Sanskrit: *skandhas*) we are made of. These elements are form (body), feelings, perceptions, mental formations, and consciousness. Our practice is to look deeply into these five elements and discover the true nature of our being—the true nature of our suffering, our happiness, our peace, our fearlessness.

———————

A Century of Spirituality

I HAVE HEARD SOME people predict that the twenty-first century will be a century of spirituality. Personally, I think it *must* be a century of spirituality if we are to survive at all. In our society, there is so much suffering, violence, despair, and confusion. There is so much fear. How can we survive without spirituality?

28

The Seeds of Happiness

WHETHER WE HAVE happiness or not depends on the seeds in our consciousness. If our seeds of compassion, understanding, and love are strong, those qualities will be able to manifest in us. If the seeds of anger, hostility, and sadness in us are strong, then we will experience much suffering.

To understand someone, we have to be aware of the quality of the seeds in his store consciousness. And we need to remember that he is not solely responsible for those seeds. His ancestors, parents, and society are coresponsible for the quality of the seeds in his consciousness. When we understand this, we are able to feel compassion for that person. With understanding and love, we will know how to water our own beautiful seeds and those of others, and we will recognize seeds of suffering and find ways to transform them.

The Art of Mindful Living

MINDFUL LIVING IS an art. You do not have to be a monk or live in a monastery to practice mindfulness. You can practice it anytime, while driving your car or doing housework. Driving in mindfulness will make the time in your car joyful, and it will also help you avoid accidents. You can use the red traffic light as a signal of mindfulness, reminding you to stop and enjoy your breathing. Similarly, when you do the dishes after dinner, you can practice mindful breathing so the time of dish washing is pleasant and meaningful. Do not feel you have to rush. If you hurry, you waste the time of dish washing. The time you spend washing dishes and doing all your other everyday tasks is precious. It is a time for being alive. When you practice mindful living, peace will bloom during your daily activities.

30

No Beginning and No End

WE USUALLY TRY to hold on to life and run away from death. But, according to the teaching, everything has been nirvana from the nonbeginning. So why do we have to grasp one thing and avoid another? In the ultimate dimension, there is no beginning and no end. We think there is something to attain, something outside of ourselves, but everything is already here.

31

Awareness of the Body

IN SITTING MEDITATION, the first thing is to be aware that you are in a sitting position. Then, you can sit in a way that brings you calm, solidity, and well-being. We can notice the position of our body in each moment, whether we are sitting, walking, standing, or lying down. We can be aware of our actions, whether we are getting up, bending down, or putting on a jacket. Awareness brings us back to ourselves, and when we are fully mindful of our body, and living in the here and now, we are in our true home.

32

Constant Transformation

IMPERMANENCE and selflessness are not negative aspects of life, but the very foundations on which life is built. Impermanence is the constant transformation of things. Without impermanence, there can be no life. Selflessness is the interdependent nature of all things. Without interdependence, nothing could exist.

———

33

The Great Insight

THIS IS THE GREAT insight of Mahayana Buddhism: *everyone* can become a buddha. What Siddhartha achieved, all of us can also achieve, whether we are a man or a woman, no matter what social class or ethnic group we were born into, or whether we practice as a monastic or as a layperson. We all have the capacity to become a fully enlightened buddha. And while on the path to becoming a fully enlightened buddha, we are all bodhisattvas.

———————

34

What the Buddha Taught

FOR FORTY-FIVE years, the Buddha said, over and over again, "I teach only suffering and the transformation of suffering." When we recognize and acknowledge our own suffering, the Buddha—which means the Buddha in us—will look at it, discover what has brought it about, and prescribe a course of action that can transform it into peace, joy, and liberation. Suffering is the means the Buddha used to liberate himself, and it is also the means by which we can become free.

35

Agonizing Questions

WHEN WE AGONIZE over questions like, "Who am I? Where do I come from? Was I wanted? What is the meaning of my life?" we suffer because we're caught in the idea of a separate self. But if we look deeply, we can practice no-self. This is the realization that we're not a separate self; we're connected to our ancestors and to all beings.

36

For All Generations

WE HAVE TO LIVE in a way that liberates the ancestors and future generations who are inside of us. Joy, peace, freedom, and harmony are not individual matters. If we do not liberate our ancestors, we will be in bondage all our life, and we will transmit that to our children and grandchildren. Now is the time to do it. To liberate them means to liberate ourselves. This is the teaching of interbeing. As long as the ancestors in us are still suffering, we cannot really be happy. If we take one step mindfully, freely, happily touching the earth, we do it for all previous and future generations. They all arrive with us at the same moment, and all of us find peace at the same time.

37

Enjoy Being a Buddha

BECOMING A BUDDHA is not so difficult. A buddha is someone who is enlightened, capable of loving, and forgiving. You know that at times you're like that. So enjoy being a buddha. When you sit, allow the Buddha in you to sit. When you walk, allow the Buddha in you to walk. Enjoy your practice. If you don't become a buddha, who will?

———————

38

Stopping Thoughts

YOU CAN NATURALLY stop your thoughts if you focus your attention fully on your in-breath and your out-
breath. After one or two minutes of practice, the quality of
your in-breath and out-breath will improve. Your breath
will become deeper, slower, and more harmonious and
peaceful, whether you are lying down, sitting, or walking.
By practicing mindful breathing, we bring the elements
of harmony and peace into our body.

39

Ghosts

DO YOU HAVE A problem right now, in this moment? Look at yourself in your physical form, your feelings, your perceptions. Do you have a problem? If we see that we don't have any problem at all in the present moment, we shouldn't let the ghosts of the past dominate us. We should not let the projections of the past or the future break us down. They're just ghosts. That's why we train ourselves to always be in the present moment. That's our practice. That's our path. It's the way to reconciliation.

40

True Practice

DEEPENING OUR PRACTICE means having a genuine practice, practicing not in form only. When your practice is genuine, it will bring joy, peace, and stability to yourself and to the people around you. Actually I prefer the phrase *true practice*. To me, the practice should be pleasant. True practice can bring life to us right away. As you practice mindful breathing, you become alive, you become real, not only when you sit or walk, but when you're making breakfast or performing any activity. If you know how to breathe in and out mindfully while making breakfast with a smile, you will cultivate freedom—freedom from thinking about the past or worrying about the future— aliveness, joy, and compassion. That is true practice, and its effect can be seen right away.

41

Nothing to Search For

WHEN WE TRANSCEND notions of inside and outside, we know that the object we wish to attain is already within us. We don't have to search for it in space or time. It is already available in the present moment. The contemplation on nonattainment is very important. The object we wish to attain is already attained. We don't need to attain anything. We already have it. We already are it.

42

The Buddha Walking

IN THE BEGINNING, we may believe that there must be someone in order for the breathing to be possible; there must be someone in order for the walking to be possible. But in fact the walking, the breathing, is enough; we don't need a walker, we don't need a breather. We can just notice that there is walking going on. There is breathing going on.

What I consider to be the Buddha walking is just the walking, but it's a high quality of walking. Because that walking is enjoyable, it's mindful walking—there's a lot of peace and joy. The Buddha is that breathing. The Buddha is that walking.

43

The Two Aspects of Buddhist Meditation

IF YOU LOOK INTO Buddhist meditation, you will find that it has two aspects: first, stopping, and then, deep looking. When you achieve stopping, you become solid and concentrated. That allows you to practice looking deeply into what's here, and looking deeply into the nature of things brings insight. This understanding will liberate you from your suffering.

44

We Already Have Enough

THE BUDDHA SPOKE about the practice of *samtusta,* recognizing that we have enough conditions to be happy right here and right now. We don't need to obtain any more. *Samtusta* has been translated as realizing that one is satisfied with little. When we go home to the present moment, we view all the conditions of happiness that we have, and we may find that they are more than enough for us to be happy right now. We need to stop running after things, because even if we get the object of our desire, we won't be happy and we'll want to run after another one.

45
The Bridge

BREATH IS THE BRIDGE that connects life to consciousness, the bridge that unites your body to your thoughts. Whenever your mind becomes scattered, use your breath as the means to take hold of your mind again.

———————

46

Deep Listening and Loving Speech

DEEP LISTENING AND loving speech are wonderful instruments to help us arrive at the kind of understanding we all need as a basis for appropriate action. You listen deeply for only one purpose—to allow the other person to empty his or her heart. This is already an act of relieving suffering. To stop any suffering, no matter how small, is a great action of peace. The path to end suffering depends on your understanding and your capacity to act without causing harm or further suffering. This is acting with compassion, your best protection.

47

The Mind of Enlightenment

BODHICHITTA (SANSKRIT) is the mind of enlightenment, beginner's mind. When we're inspired by the desire to practice and transform our suffering so we can help the many people around us who suffer, the mind of that moment is very beautiful. It's the mind of a bodhisattva, one who attains his or her own liberation in order to help all beings. Sometimes we call it the "mind of love." It's because of love that we practice. We're not just trying to run away from suffering. We want more than that. We want to transform our own suffering and be free in order to help many other people to transform their suffering.

48

Enjoy a Moment of Nothing

IF YOU CAN FIND a moment to sit, wherever you are, stay there and enjoy doing nothing. Just enjoy your in-breath and out-breath. Don't allow yourself to be carried away by your thinking, worries, or projects. Just sit there and enjoy doing nothing; enjoy your breathing and the fact that you are alive and that you have twenty minutes or half an hour to enjoy doing nothing. This is very healing, transforming, and nourishing.

———————

49

What Is a Leaf?

SUPPOSE I HOLD a leaf in my hand. What do you see? A leaf is a leaf; it is not a flower. But in fact, when we look deeply into the leaf, we can see many things. We can see the plant, we can see the sunshine, we can see the clouds, we can see the earth. When we utter the word *leaf,* we have to be aware that a leaf is made of non-leaf elements. If we remove the non-leaf elements, such as the sunshine, the clouds, and the soil, there will be no leaf left. So it is with our bodies and ourselves. We're not the same as, nor are we separate from, other beings. We're connected to everything, and everything is alive.

50

The Basic Principle

HAVE WE WASTED OUR HOURS AND our days? Are we wasting our lives? These are important questions. Practicing Buddhism is to be alive in each moment. When we practice sitting or walking, we have the means to do it perfectly. During the rest of the day, we also practice. It is more difficult, but it is possible. The sitting and the walking must be extended to the non-walking, non-sitting moments of our day. That is the basic principle of meditation.

Subtle Gestures

A ZEN MASTER observes the student in silence, while the student tries to bring the practice into every moment of life. The student may feel that she is not receiving enough attention, but her ways and acts cannot escape the observation of the master. The master can see if the student is or is not "awake."

If, for example, the student shuts the door noisily or carelessly, she is demonstrating a lack of mindfulness. Closing the door gently is not in itself a virtuous act, but awareness of the fact that you are closing the door is an expression of real practice. In this case, the master simply reminds the student to close the door gently, to be mindful. The master does this not only to respect the quiet of the monastery, but to point out to the student that she was not practicing mindfulness, that her acts were not majestic or subtle. It is said in Buddhism that there are ninety thousand "subtle gestures" to practice. These gestures and acts are expressions of the presence of mindfulness.

52

Easily Hurt

As CHILDREN, we were very vulnerable. We got hurt very easily. A stern look from our father could make us unhappy. A strong word from our mother could cause a wound in our heart. As young children, we have a lot of feelings but it's difficult to express ourselves. We try and try. Sometimes, even if we can find the words, the adults around us can't hear us, don't listen, or won't allow us to talk.

We can go home to ourselves and talk to our little child, listen to our child, and respond directly to him. I myself have done this, even though I received love and care from my parents. This practice has helped me tremendously. The child is still there and may be deeply wounded. We have neglected the child in us for a long time. We have to come back, and comfort, love, and care for the child within us.

53

When You Argue with the One You Love

WHEN YOU GET into an argument with someone you love, please close your eyes and visualize yourself three hundred years from now. When you open your eyes, you will only want to take each other in your arms and acknowledge how precious each of you is. The teaching of impermanence helps us appreciate fully what is there, without attachment or forgetfulness.

54
Rites of Life

CHOPPING WOOD IS meditation. Carrying water is meditation. Be mindful twenty-four hours a day, not just during the one hour you may allot for formal meditation, or reading scripture and reciting prayers. Each act must be carried out in mindfulness. Each act is a rite, a ceremony. Raising your cup of tea to your mouth is a rite. Does the word *rite* seem too solemn? I use that word in order to jolt you into the realization of the life-and-death matter of awareness.

55

The Real Miracle

I LIKE TO WALK alone on country paths, rice plants and wild grasses on both sides, putting each foot down on the earth in mindfulness, knowing that I walk on the wondrous earth. In such moments, existence is a miraculous and mysterious reality. People usually consider walking on water or in thin air a miracle. But I think the real miracle is not to walk either on water or in thin air, but to walk on the earth. Every day we are engaged in a miracle that we don't even recognize: a blue sky, white clouds, green leaves, the black, curious eyes of a child—our own two eyes. All is a miracle.

56

Stop the War

THE INSIGHT OF nonduality will put a stop to the war in you. You have struggled in the past, and perhaps you are still struggling—but is it necessary? No. Struggle is useless. Stop struggling.

57

The Future Is Now

THE PRACTICE OF mindfulness doesn't forbid us to plan for the future. It's best not to lose ourselves in uncertainty and fear over the future, but if we're truly established in the present moment, we can bring the future to the here and the now, and make plans. We're not losing the present moment when we think about the future. In fact, the present moment contains both past and future. The only material that the future is made of is the present. If you know how to handle the present in the best way you can, that's all you can do for the future. Handling the present moment with all your attention, all your intelligence, is already building a future.

———————

58

Inner Silence

SILENCE IS SOMETHING that comes from your heart, not from outside. Silence doesn't mean not talking and not doing things; it means that you are not disturbed inside, there is no talking inside. If you're truly silent, then no matter what situation you find yourself in, you can enjoy the silence. There are moments when you think you're silent and all around is silent, but talking is going on all the time inside your head. That's not silence. The practice is to find silence in all the activities you do.

59

Children of the Earth

WE ARE CHILDREN of the earth. We rely on the earth, and the earth relies on us. Whether the earth is beautiful, fresh, and green, or arid and parched, depends on our way of walking. Please touch the earth in mindfulness, with joy and concentration. The earth will heal you, and you will heal the earth.

60

The Liberating Power of Insight

CONCENTRATION HELPS us focus on just one thing. With concentration, the energy of looking becomes more powerful, and insight is possible. Insight always has the power of liberating us. If mindfulness is there, and we know how to keep mindfulness alive, concentration will be there, too. And if we know how to keep concentration alive, insight will also come. The energy of mindfulness enables us to look deeply and gain the insight we need so that transformation is possible.

61

A Game of Hide-and-Seek

HAVE YOU EVER PLAYED with a kaleidoscope? Just a small movement is enough to make something miraculous appear. A tableau of colors and forms is presented to you, a manifestation. You keep this view for a few seconds, then you turn the kaleidoscope and another manifestation appears. Should we cry every time one of these manifestations comes to an end? A flower manifests, then disappears, then manifests, then disappears—thousands upon thousands of times. If you look deeply at things, you will see this reality. We manifest, then disappear. It is a game of hide-and-seek.

62

Are You Sure?

ALL OF US ARE only human, and we have wrong perceptions every day. Our spouse or partner is also subject to wrong perceptions, so we must help each other to see more clearly and more deeply. We should not trust our perceptions too much—that is something the Buddha taught. "Are you sure of your perceptions?" he asked us. I urge you to write this phrase down on a card and put it up on the wall of your room: "Are you sure of your perceptions?"

There is a river of perceptions in you. You should sit down on the bank of this river and contemplate your perceptions. Most of our perceptions, the Buddha said, are false. Are you sure of your perceptions? This question is addressed to you. It is a bell of mindfulness.

63

A Gift to the One You Love

WHEN YOU KNOW how to generate your own presence, you can make a gift of it to the one you love. This is something very practical. It is easy to do, it costs nothing, and it can be done very quickly. You do not have to practice for years to see the results. One minute will do. So you should put what you have learned into practice right away.

64

Walking in the Kingdom of God

WE ALL HAVE the ability to walk in the Kingdom of God, to walk in the Pure Land of Buddha, every day. You have all you need—legs, lungs, eyes, and mind—and with a little bit of practice, you can generate the energy of mindfulness within you, just like lighting a lamp. Once you have become truly alive, take a step and you will enter the Kingdom of God.

———

65

Don't Underestimate Yourself

DON'T UNDERESTIMATE yourself. You have the ability to wake up. You have the ability to be compassionate. You just need a little bit of practice to be able to touch the best that is in you. Enlightenment, mindfulness, understanding, and compassion are in you. Very simple practices—such as meditative walking, mindful breathing, or washing dishes mindfully—make it possible for you to leave hell and touch the positive seeds that are within you.

———————

66

Everyone Will Benefit

IF WE ARE NOT happy, if we are not peaceful, we can't share peace and happiness with others, even those we love, those who live under the same roof. If we are peaceful, if we are happy, we can smile and blossom like a flower, and everyone in our family, our entire society, will benefit from our peace.

———————

67

True Understanding

THE PRACTICE OF meditation is to look at reality in such a way that the boundary between subject and object will no longer be there. We have to remove the boundary between the inquirer and the object of inquiry. If we want to understand someone, we put ourselves into his skin. In order for friends or families to really understand each other, they need to become each other. The only way to understand fully is to become the object of our understanding. True understanding happens when we dismantle the barrier between the object of understanding and the subject of understanding.

68

Nondiscrimination

PEACE AND COMPASSION go hand in hand with understanding and nondiscrimination. We choose one thing over another when we discriminate. With the eyes of compassion, we can look at all of living reality at once. A compassionate person sees himself or herself in every being. With the ability to view reality from many viewpoints, we can overcome all viewpoints and act compassionately in each situation.

69

Suddenly You Are Free

YOU CAN MAKE A step and touch the earth in such a way that you establish yourself in the present moment, and you will arrive in the here and the now. You don't need to make any effort at all. Your foot touches the earth mindfully, and you arrive firmly in the here and the now. And suddenly you are free—free from all projects, all worries, all expectations. You are fully present, fully alive, and you are touching the earth.

———

The Miraculous Smile

IN OUR FACE THERE are dozens of muscles, and when we're angry or afraid, those muscles hold a lot of tension. But if we know to breathe in and be aware of them, and breathe out and smile to them, we can help them release the tension. Our face can be completely different after one in-breath and out-breath. A smile can bring a miracle.

71

Habit Energy

HABIT ENERGY IS pushing us; it pushes us to do things without our being aware. Sometimes we do something without knowing we're doing it. Even when we don't want to do something, we still do it. Sometimes we say, "I didn't want to do it, but it's stronger than me, it pushed me." So that is a seed, a habit energy, which may have come from many generations in the past.

We have inherited a lot. With mindfulness, we can become aware of the habit energy that has been passed down to us. We might see that our parents or grandparents were also very weak in ways similar to us. We can be aware without judgment that our negative habits come from these ancestral roots. We can smile at our shortcomings, at our habit energy. With awareness, we have a choice; we can act another way. We can end the cycle of suffering right now.

———————

72

You Are Safe Now

ALL KINDS OF desires are the continuation of our original desire to be safe. The little child in us continues to worry and be fearful. In the present moment there's no problem, no threat. If we don't have a problem in the present moment, it means we don't have a problem. Why continue to worry and be fearful? We have to transmit that wisdom to the inner child. We need to let the child within us know that he or she no longer has to be afraid.

73

The Anchor

THERE ARE MANY ways to come back to the here and the now, and to touch life deeply. But they all involve mindful breathing. If we're anchored in our mindful breathing, we can practice anytime. Otherwise we risk missing our lives, our lives that are lived in the here and now.

———————

74

Caught in the Idea of a Self

WESTERN PSYCHOTHERAPY AIMS at helping create a self that is stable and wholesome. But because psychotherapy in the West is still caught in the idea of self, it can bring about only a little transformation and a little healing; it can't go very far. As long as we are caught in the idea of a separate self, ignorance is still in us. When we see the intimate relationship between what is self and what is not self, ignorance is healed and suffering, anger, jealousy, and fear disappear. If we can practice no-self, we'll be able to go beyond the questions that make people suffer so much.

75

Your True Nature

WHEN WE LOOK deeply at our own nature, we can get in touch with its ultimate reality. This ultimate nature is free of birth, free of death, free from any notion such as high, low, this, that, and so forth. In Buddhism, we call this "nirvana," or "suchness." Nirvana is the extinction of all concepts, such as existence, nonexistence, death, and birth.

You have this dimension called the "ultimate" within you. In fact, you are free from birth and from death, free from existence and from nonexistence. Your true nature is the nature of nirvana. If you are from the Christian tradition, you could say that this ultimate dimension is God. The Kingdom of God is free from birth and death, free from high and low, free from existence and nonexistence.

76

Saints

SOMETIMES YOU ENCOUNTER people who are so pure, beautiful, and content. They give you the impression that they are divine, that they actually are saints or holy beings. What you perceive in them is their awakened self, their Buddha nature, and what they reflect back to you is your own capacity for being awake.

The Most Wonderful Moment of Your Life

THE TEACHING OF the Buddha tells you clearly and plainly to make this the most magnificent and wonderful moment of your life. This present moment must become the most wonderful moment in your life. All you need to transform this present moment into a wonderful one is freedom. All you need to do is free yourself from your worries and preoccupations about the past, the future, and so on.

———————

78

The Wounded Child

WHEN WE SPEAK of listening with compassion, we usually think of listening to someone else. But we must also listen to the wounded child inside of us. Sometimes the wounded child in us needs all our attention. That little child might emerge from the depths of your consciousness and ask for your attention. If you are mindful, you will hear his or her voice calling for help. At that moment, instead of paying attention to whatever is in front of you, go back and tenderly embrace the wounded child.

79

Releasing Our Cows

ONE DAY THE Buddha was sitting in the forest with a number of monks when a peasant came by. He had just lost his cows; they had run away. He asked the monks whether they had seen his cows passing by. The Buddha said, "No, we haven't seen your cows passing through here; you may want to look for them in another direction."

When the farmer had gone, the Buddha turned to his monks, smiled, and said, "Dear friends, you should be very happy. You don't have any cows to lose."

One practice we can do is to take a piece of paper and write down the names of our cows. Then we can look deeply to see whether we're capable of releasing some of them. We may have thought these things were crucial to our well-being, but if we look deeply, we may realize that they are the obstacles to our true joy and happiness.

80

The Universal Seed

MINDFULNESS IS the kind of light that shows us the way. It is the living Buddha inside of each of us. Mindfulness gives birth to insight, awakening, compassion, and love. Not only Buddhists, but also Christians, Jews, Muslims, and Marxists can accept that each of us has the capacity of being mindful, that everyone has the seed of mindfulness in himself or herself. If we know how to water this seed, it will grow, and we will become alive again, capable of enjoying all the wonders of life.

81

Don't Run Away

THE TENDENCY TO run away from suffering is there in every one of us. We think that by seeking pleasure we'll avoid suffering. But this doesn't work. It stunts our growth and our happiness. Happiness isn't possible without understanding, compassion, and love. And love is not possible if we don't understand our suffering and the other person's suffering.

Getting in touch with suffering will help us cultivate compassion and love. Without understanding and love we can't be happy, and we can't make other people happy. We all have the seeds of compassion, forgiveness, joy, and nonfear in us. If we're constantly trying to avoid suffering, there is no way for these seeds to grow.

82

Something to Believe In

MINDFULNESS IS something we can believe in. To believe in mindfulness is safe, and not at all abstract. When we drink a glass of water and know that we are drinking a glass of water, mindfulness is there. When we sit, walk, stand, or breathe, and know that we are sitting, walking, standing, or breathing, we touch the seed of mindfulness in us, and after a few days, our mindfulness will grow quite strong.

———

A Deeper View of Life

THE WORK OF acknowledging everything in mindfulness leads us to a deeper view of what life is. It is very important to understand that impermanence is not a negative aspect of life. Impermanence is the very basis of life. If what exists were not impermanent, no life could continue. If a grain of corn were not impermanent, it could not become a corn plant. If a tiny child were not impermanent, she could not grow into an adult.

Life is impermanent, but that does not mean that it is not worth living. It is precisely because of its impermanence that we value life so dearly. Therefore we must know how to live each moment deeply and use it in a responsible way. If we are able to live the present moment completely, we will not feel regret later. We will know how to care for those who are close to us and how to bring them happiness. When we accept that all things are impermanent, we will not be incapacitated by suffering when things decay and die. We can remain peaceful and content in the face of continuity and change, prosperity and decline, success and failure.

84

Conscious Breathing

BREATHING AND knowing that we are breathing is a basic practice. No one can be truly successful in the art of meditating without going through the door of breathing. To practice conscious breathing is to open the door to stopping and looking deeply in order to enter the domain of concentration and insight. The meditation master Tang Hoi said that *Anapanasati* [being aware of breathing] is the great vehicle offered by the Buddha to living beings.

Conscious breathing is the way into any sort of meditative concentration. Conscious breathing also leads us to the basic realization of the impermanence, emptiness, interdependent origination, selflessness, and nonduality of all that is. It is true that we can practice stopping and looking deeply without using conscious breathing, but conscious breathing is the safest and surest path we can follow.

85

Mind and Body as One

WHEN BODY AND mind are together, you are fully present. You are fully alive and you can touch the wonders of life that are available in the here and the now. So you practice not only with your mind but with your body. Body and mind should be experienced as one thing, not two. On that ground, you see that everything you are looking for is already there.

———————

86

Everything We Do Brings Joy

BRUSHING OUR teeth, cooking our breakfast, walking to the meditation hall—everything we do, every step, every breath should bring joy and happiness to us. Life is already full of suffering; we don't need to create more.

87

The Ocean

SUPPOSE WE ARE looking at the ocean. On the surface we see waves rising and falling. From the point of view of the waves, there is birth and death, high and low, rising and falling. There are distinctions between waves.

But each wave is made of a substance called "water." It is a wave, but at the same time, it is water. Concepts such as birth and death, higher and lower, rising and falling apply only to the waves, which represent the historical dimension, and do not apply to the water itself, the ultimate dimension.

———————

88

The Deepest Relief

WE COME TO the practice of meditation seeking relief from our suffering, and meditation can teach us how to transform our suffering and obtain basic relief. But the deepest kind of relief is the realization of nirvana.

———————

89

An Invitation from the Buddha

WE LIVE IN A TIME when everyone is too caught up in the preoccupations of everyday life, and we do not have enough time to live in suchness, with mindfulness. We do not take the time to touch things in depth, to discover the true nature of life. You are invited to use your intelligence, your time, and your resources to taste this timeless meditation that was handed down to us by our original teacher, the Buddha.

90

Remember Their Impermanence

WHEN WE CAN envision the death of one we love, we are able to let go of anger and reproachfulness toward that person. We learn to live in a sweeter way with those we love, to look after them and to make them happy. Our awareness of impermanence keeps thoughtless words and actions about those we love from invading our daily lives. We learn how to avoid hurting the ones most important to us, and avoid sowing seeds of suffering in ourselves and in them.

———————

The Practice of Nonpractice

IF YOU STRUGGLE during your sitting meditation or walking meditation, you are not doing it right. The Buddha said, "My practice is the practice of nonpractice." That means a lot. Give up all struggle. Allow yourself to be, to rest.

92

Don't Take Sides

RECONCILIATION MEANS leaving behind our dualistic view and our tendency to want to punish the other person. Reconciliation opposes all forms of ambition, but reconciliation doesn't take sides. Most of us want to take sides in a conflict. We distinguish right from wrong based on partial evidence or hearsay. We think we need indignation in order to act. But even legitimate, righteous indignation isn't enough. Our world doesn't lack people who are willing to throw themselves into action! What we need are people who are capable of loving and not taking sides so that they can embrace the whole of reality.

We have to continue to practice mindfulness and reconciliation until we can see the bodies of hungry children as our own, until the pain in the bodies of all species is our own. Then we will have realized nondiscrimination, real love. Then we can look at all beings with the eyes of compassion, and we can do the real work of helping to alleviate suffering.

93

The Spiritual Dimension

WE HAVE TO practice peace in our corporations, our cities, and our schools. Schoolteachers have to practice peace, and teach their students how to practice peace. The presidents of countries or the heads of political parties must practice peace, must pray for peace in their body and mind, before they can be effective in asking other prime ministers and heads of state to join them in making peace. Ideally each peace conference would begin with walking meditation and sitting meditation. And someone would be there to guide the total relaxation in order to remove tension, anger, and fear in body and mind. That is bringing the spiritual dimension into our political and social life.

94

Limitless Life

A MULTITUDE OF phenomena is present in our life, just as we ourselves are present in many different phenomena. We are life, and life is limitless. Perhaps one can say that we are only alive when we live the life of the world, and so live the sufferings and joys of others. The suffering of others is our own suffering, and the happiness of others is our own happiness. If our life has no limits, the assembly of the five aggregates (*skandhas*) that makes up our self also has no limits. The impermanent character of the universe, the successes and failures of life, can no longer manipulate us. When you have seen the reality of interdependence and entered deeply into its reality, nothing can oppress you any longer.

95

What Is Your True Face?

WE CANNOT SAY the Buddha is alive or dead. Reality transcends birth, death, production, and destruction. "What was your face before your parents were born?" This is an invitation to find your true self that isn't subject to birth and death.

96

Generations of Suffering

WITH PRACTICE, WE can see that our wounded child is not only us. Our wounded child may represent several generations. Our mother may have suffered throughout her life. Our father may have suffered. Perhaps our parents weren't able to look after the wounded child in themselves. So when we're embracing the wounded child in us, we're embracing all the wounded children of our past generations. This practice is not a practice for ourselves alone, but for numberless generations of ancestors and descendants.

97

A Solid Reality

WHEN YOU BREATHE in, you bring all of yourself together, body and mind; you become one. Equipped with
that energy of mindfulness and concentration, you may
take a step. And if you can take one mindful step, you can
take another and another. You have the insight that this is
your true home—you are alive, you are fully present, you
are touching life as a reality. Your true home is a solid reality that you can touch with your feet, with your hands,
and with your mind.

98

Live Vigorously

MINDFULNESS PRACTICE is not an evasion or an escape. It means entering vigorously into life—with the strength generated by the energy of mindfulness. Without this freedom and concentration, there is no happiness.

99

Like a Pebble in the River

PLEASE, WHEN YOU practice meditation, don't make any effort. Allow yourself to be like a pebble at rest. The pebble is resting at the bottom of the river, and the pebble does not have to do anything. While you are walking, you are resting. While you are sitting, you are resting.

———————

Nothing to Attain

THE *HEART SUTRA* says that there is "nothing to attain." We meditate not to attain enlightenment, because enlightenment is already in us. We don't have to search anywhere. We don't need a purpose or a goal. We don't practice in order to obtain some high position. In aimlessness, we see that we do not lack anything, that we already are what we want to become, and our striving just comes to a halt. We are at peace in the present moment, just seeing the sunlight streaming through our window or hearing the sound of the rain. We don't have to run after anything. We can enjoy every moment. People talk about entering nirvana, but we are already there. Aimlessness and nirvana are one.

101

This Is Your Time

THIS IS YOUR OWN time. This spot where you sit is your own spot. It is on this very spot and in this very moment that you can become enlightened. You don't have to sit beneath a special tree in a distant land. Practice like this for a few months, and you will begin to know a profound and renewing delight.

———————

102

Like the Moon in the Sky

WE SHOULD BE free to experience the happiness that just comes to us without our having to seek it. If you are a free person, happiness can come over you just like that! Look at the moon. It travels in the sky completely free, and this freedom produces beauty and happiness. I am convinced that happiness is not possible unless it is based on freedom. If you are a free woman, if you are a free man, you will enjoy happiness. But if you are a slave, even if only the slave of an idea, happiness will be very difficult for you to achieve. That is why you should cultivate freedom, including freedom from your own concepts and ideas. Let go of your ideas, even if abandoning them is not easy.

A Garden of Poems

ONE DAY IN New York City, I met a Buddhist scholar and I told her about my practice of mindfulness in the vegetable garden. I enjoy growing lettuce, tomatoes, and other vegetables, and I like to spend time gardening every day.

She said, "You shouldn't spend your time growing vegetables. You should spend more time writing poems. Your poems are so beautiful. Everyone can grow lettuce, but not everyone can write poems like you do."

I told her, "If I don't grow lettuce, I can't write poems."

104

The Stream of Life

IF WE LOOK INTO one cell of our body or one cell of our consciousness, we recognize the presence of all the generations of ancestors in us. Our ancestors are not only human beings. Before human beings appeared, we were other species. We have been trees, plants, grasses, minerals, a squirrel, a deer, a monkey, and one-celled animals. All these generations of ancestors are present in each cell of our body and mind. We are the continuation of this stream of life.

In the Here, In the Now

BREATHING IN, repeat "In the here, in the here." Breathing out, repeat "In the now, in the now." Although these are different words, they mean exactly the same thing: I have arrived in the here. I have arrived in the now. I am home in the here. I am home in the now.

When you practice like that, you practice stopping. Stopping is the basic Buddhist practice of meditation. You stop running. You stop struggling. You allow yourself to rest, to heal, to calm.

106

Worrying

YES, THERE IS tremendous suffering all over the world, but knowing this need not paralyze us. If we practice mindful breathing, mindful walking, mindful sitting, and working in mindfulness, we try our best to help, and we can have peace in our heart. Worrying does not accomplish anything. Even if you worry twenty times more, it will not change the situation of the world. In fact, your anxiety will only make things worse. Even though things are not as we would like, we can still be content, knowing we are trying our best and will continue to do so. If we don't know how to breathe, smile, and live every moment of our life deeply, we will never be able to help anyone.

———

107

Water the Right Seeds

THE SEEDS OF negativity are always there, but very positive seeds also exist, such as the seeds of compassion, tolerance, and love. These seeds are all there in the soil, but without rain they cannot manifest. Our practice is to recognize and water the positive seeds. If you recognize the seed of compassion in yourself, you should make sure that it is watered several times every day.

108

More Difficult to Cure

IF WE'RE AWARE that the self is always made of nonself elements, we will never be enslaved by or afraid of the notion of self or nonself. But if the notion of self is harmful or dangerous, the notion of nonself may be even more dangerous. Clinging to the notion of self is not good, but clinging to the notion of nonself is worse because it is more difficult to cure.

———————

A Mindful Breakfast

EVEN A DAILY HABIT like eating breakfast, when done as a practice, can be powerful. It generates the energy of mindfulness and concentration that makes life authentic. When we prepare breakfast, breakfast making can also be a practice. We can be really alive, fully present, and very happy during breakfast making. We can see making breakfast as mundane work or as a privilege—it just depends on our way of looking. The cold water is available. The hot water is available. The soap is available. The kettle is available. The fire is available. The food is available. Everything is there to make our happiness a possibility.

Empty of What?

EMPTINESS ALWAYS means empty of something. A cup is empty of water. A bowl is empty of soup. We are empty of a separate, independent self. We cannot be by ourselves alone. We can only inter-be with everything else in the cosmos. The practice is to nourish the insight into emptiness all day long. Wherever we go, we touch the nature of emptiness in everything we contact. We look deeply at the table, the blue sky, our friend, the mountain, the river, our anger, and our happiness, and see that these are all empty of a separate self. When we touch these things deeply, we see the interbeing and interpenetrating nature of all that is. Emptiness does not mean nonexistence. It means interdependent coarising, impermanence, and nonself.

III

Taking Care of the Future

THE FUTURE IS being made out of the present, so the best way to take care of the future is to take care of the present moment. This is logical and clear. Spending a lot of time speculating and worrying about the future is totally useless. We can only take care of our future by taking care of the present moment, because the future is made out of only one substance: the present. Only if you are anchored in the present can you prepare well for the future.

———————

Direct to You from the Buddha

"BREATHING IN, I know that I am breathing in." Let me remind you that this practice comes to us directly from the Buddha. You are free of any intention to judge, find fault, reject, or cling, and you maintain that freedom in relation to whatever is happening. When you get angry or depressed, it is the same. You simply recognize what is there—anger, depression, and so forth—without any sense of disapproval or rejection. If you recognize emotion as existing in the moment, you will not feel upset. There is no battle to win or lose—this is Buddhist meditation.

113

The Beautiful Earth

THE EARTH IS so beautiful. We are beautiful also. We can allow ourselves to walk mindfully, touching the earth, our wonderful mother, with each step. We don't need to wish our friends, "Peace be with you." Peace is already with them. We only need to help them cultivate the habit of touching peace in each moment.

———————

114

When Mind Is Elsewhere

IN OUR DAILY LIFE, we lose ourselves all the time. The body is here, but the mind is somewhere else—in the past, in the future, carried away by anger, jealousy, fear, and so on. The mind is not really present with the body. We are not really here.

To be truly here, we have to bring the body back to the mind, and the mind back to the body. We have to bring about what is called the "unity of body and mind." This is very important in Buddhist meditation. Often, the body and the mind go in different directions, and so we are not fully here. Therefore, we have to do what is necessary for them to come back together again. Buddhism teaches us methods for doing this, such as mindfulness of the breath.

115

Be a Happy Formation

THE "I" IS MADE up of the body and mind (*namarupa* in Sanskrit). The physical form is body, and all the other elements (*skandhas*) are mind. When we look deeply into these five elements, we do not see any absolute, permanent identity. They are impermanent. If you practice in such a way that harmony is established in the realm of the five elements, then joy, peace, and happiness will be possible. Through breathing, through bringing your mind back to your body, through the method of deep looking, you will reestablish harmony and peace in the realm of the five elements. You will become a happy formation, pleasing to encounter, and you will be able to bring happiness to the living beings around you.

116

Be Worthy of Your Food

IN MY MONASTIC TRADITION, we practice the Five Contemplations before eating. The second Contemplation is, "May we eat with mindfulness and gratitude so as to be worthy to receive this food." I think the best way to make ourselves worthy of this food is to eat it mindfully. The whole cosmos has come together to make this food available, and someone has spent an hour or more preparing the food. It would be a pity if we didn't eat it in mindfulness.

———————

117

Still Water

HAVE YOU EVER seen yourself in a mirror that distorts the image? Your face is long, your eyes are huge, and your legs are really short. Don't be like that mirror. It is better to be like the still water on the mountain lake. We often do not reflect things clearly, and we suffer because of our wrong perceptions. When we see things or listen to other people, we often don't see clearly or really listen. We see and hear our projections and our prejudices.

We need to make our water still if we want to receive reality as it is. If you feel agitated, don't do or say anything. Just breathe in and out until you are calm enough. Then ask your friend to repeat what he has said. This will avoid a lot of damage. Stillness is the foundation of understanding and insight. Stillness is strength.

118

Opening the Door of Communication

TO MEDITATE IS to look deeply into the nature of things, including our own nature and the nature of the person in front of us. When we see the true nature of that person, we discover his or her difficulties, aspirations, suffering, and anxieties. We can sit down, hold our partner's hand, look deeply at him, and say, "Darling, do I understand you enough? Do I water your seeds of suffering? Do I water your seeds of joy? Please tell me how I can love you better." If we say this from the bottom of our heart, he may begin to cry, and that is a good sign. It means the door of communication may be opening.

119

Freedom from Despair

FREEDOM IS THE basis of all happiness. Without freedom, there is no happiness. This means freedom from despair, freedom from resentment, freedom from jealousy and fear. Genuine practice is practice that helps you become freer and more solid. Every step you take, every breath you take, every minute of sitting meditation, and every bowl you wash should give you more solidity and freedom.

Mindfulness of the Mind

TO TAKE HOLD of your mind, you must practice mindfulness of the mind. You must know how to observe and recognize the presence of every feeling and thought that arises in you. The Zen master Thuong Chieu wrote, "If the practitioner knows his own mind clearly, he will obtain results with little effort. But if he does not know anything about his own mind, all of his effort will be wasted." If you want to know your own mind, there is only one way: to observe and recognize everything about it. This must be done at all times, during your day-to-day life no less than during the hour of meditation.

121

The External World

EVERY OBJECT of the mind is itself mind.

———————

Tasting True Liberation

EVERYONE WE CHERISH will, someday, get sick and die. If we do not practice the meditation on emptiness, when those things happen, we will be overwhelmed. Concentration on emptiness is a way of staying in touch with life as it is, but it has to be practiced and not just talked about. We observe our body and see all the causes and conditions that have brought it to be—our parents, our country, the air, and even future generations. We go beyond time and space, me and mine, and taste true liberation. If we only study emptiness as a philosophy, it will not be a door of liberation. Emptiness is a door of liberation when we penetrate it deeply, and we realize interdependent coarising and the interbeing nature of everything that is.

123

Our Mother

OUR MOTHER IS the person who first teaches us love, the most important subject in life. Without my mother, I could never have known how to love. Thanks to her, I can love my neighbors. Thanks to her, I can love all living beings. Through her, I acquired my first notions of understanding and compassion. Mother is the foundation of all love, and many religious traditions recognize this and pay deep honor to a maternal figure, such as the Virgin Mary or the goddess Kuan Yin. An infant barely has to open her mouth to cry before her mother is already running to the cradle. Mother is a gentle and sweet spirit who makes unhappiness and worries disappear. When the word *mother* is uttered, already we feel our heart overflowing with love.

———————

124

Nourish Yourself

THE BUDDHA advises us to create the feeling of joy and happiness in order to nourish ourselves before we deal with the painful feelings. Just as a surgeon may judge that a patient is too weak to undergo surgery, and recommend that the patient first get some rest and nourishment so she can bear the surgery, so we need to strengthen our foundation of joy and happiness before focusing on our suffering.

Orange Meditation

TAKE THE TIME to eat an orange in mindfulness. If you eat an orange in forgetfulness, caught in your anxiety and sorrow, the orange is not really there. But if you bring your mind and body together to produce true presence, you can see that the orange is a miracle. Peel the orange. Smell the fruit. See the orange blossoms in the orange, and the rain and the sun that have gone through the orange blossoms. The orange tree has taken several months to bring this wonder to you. Put a section in your mouth, close your mouth mindfully, and with mindfulness feel the juice coming out of the orange. Taste the sweetness. Do you have the time to do so? If you think you don't have time to eat an orange like this, what are you using that time for? Are you using your time to worry, or using your time to live?

126

Mental Formations

IN THE PRACTICE of Buddhism, we see that all mental formations—such as compassion, love, fear, sorrow, and despair—are organic in nature. We don't need to be afraid of them, because transformation is possible. Just by having this deep insight into the organic nature of mental formations, you become a lot more solid, a lot calmer and more peaceful. With just a smile, and mindful breathing, you can start to transform them.

The Pleasures of Practice

THE PRACTICE SHOULD be enjoyable and pleasant. The elements called "joy" and "pleasure," *mudita* and *priti* in Sanskrit, are a very important part of meditation. If you are suffering during meditation, your practice is not correct. Practice should be enjoyable and pleasant. It should be full of joy.

128

Peace Is Contagious

IF YOU HAVE BEEN able to embrace your in-breath and your out-breath with tenderness, you know that they in turn embrace your body and your mind. If you have practiced meditation, you have already discovered this. Peace is contagious. Happiness is also contagious.

———————

Take Back Your Sovereignty

AFTER WALKING mindfully for a few minutes, you will see that you are much more solid. The past and the future can no longer grab you and pull you away from life. As a result, you are much more yourself. You have more sovereignty. Taking back your sovereignty is the practice. You are more solid and more free.

Appreciating Simple Joys

PLEASE TAKE the hand of your little boy or little girl and walk slowly to the park. You may be surprised to notice that while you are enjoying the sunshine, the trees, and the birds, your child feels a little bored. Young people today get bored easily. They are used to television, handheld video games, war toys, loud music, and other kinds of excitement. We adults too try to fill our loneliness with these kinds of things, and all of us suffer.

We have to teach ourselves and our children how to appreciate the simple joys that are available. This may not be easy in our complex, distracted society, but it is essential for our survival. Sitting on the grass with your little boy or girl, point out the tiny yellow and blue flowers that grow among the grasses, and contemplate these miracles together. Peace education begins on this occasion.

Human Progress

IF THE HUMAN species has been able to make any progress, it is because of our heart of love and compassion. We need to learn from compassionate beings how to develop the practice of deep observation for the sake of others. Then others will be able to learn from us the way to live in the present, and see the impermanent and selfless nature of all that is. This insight will lighten suffering.

Unlocking the Door of Reality

THE TEACHINGS OF impermanence and nonself were offered by the Buddha as keys to unlock the door of reality. We have to train ourselves to look in a way so that we know when we touch one thing, we touch everything. We have to see that the one is in the all, and the all is in the one. We touch not only the phenomenal aspects of reality but the ground of being. Things are impermanent and without self. They have to undergo birth and death. But if we touch them very deeply, we touch the ground of being that is free from birth and death, free from permanence and impermanence, self and nonself.

Where the Buddhas Live

THE ADDRESS OF the buddhas and the bodhisattvas is "here and now." That is the address of happiness, the address of life. The Buddha said, "Life is accessible only in the present moment." Life with all its wonders is accessible right now. So we train in coming back to the present moment. When you are sitting on your meditation cushion, you are established in the present moment. At that moment, you touch life deeply. During walking meditation, you do the same thing. Each step brings you back to your true home, the home of your spiritual ancestors— the present moment. It is in the present moment that life, peace, joy, happiness, and well-being are possible.

134
Our Children

WE ARE IN our children. We have transmitted ourselves entirely to them. Our sons, our daughters are our continuation. Our son, our daughter *is* us. And they will carry us far into the future. If we have the time to love our children with compassion and understanding, they will benefit from that and make the future better for themselves, their children, and future generations.

———

135

As Concentration Grows

IF WE ARE concentrated, life is deep, and we have more joy and stability. We can drive mindfully, we can cut carrots mindfully, we can shower mindfully. When we do things this way, concentration grows. When concentration grows, we gain insight into our life.

136

Feed Your Love, Not Your Suffering

NOTHING CAN survive without food, not even suffering. No animal or plant can survive without food. In order for our love to survive, we have to feed it. If we don't feed it, or we feed it the wrong kind of nutrients, our love will die. In a short time, our love can turn into hate. Our suffering, our depression also needs food to survive. If our depression refuses to go away, it's because we keep feeding it daily. We can look deeply into the source of nutrition that is feeding our suffering.

Images of the Past

IF WE HAVE BEEN abused as a child, almost anything we see or hear can bring us back to that image of being abused. Being so constantly in touch with these images of the past can give rise to feelings of fear, anger, and despair. We call this "inappropriate attention" (Sanskrit: *ayoniso manaskara*) because it takes us away from the present moment and into a place of old suffering. It's very important that whenever our attention is brought to that place, to that kind of image, we have ways of dealing with the sorrow, fear, and suffering that arise.

When suffering arises, our practice is to breathe in and out, and say, "Breathing in, I know that suffering is in me." Recognizing and embracing the mental formation is our practice. With the energy of mindfulness, we recognize that our old suffering is only an image; it's not reality. And we can see that life with all its wonders is here, that living happily in the present moment is possible, and then we can change the whole situation.

138

I Think, Therefore . . .

DESCARTES SAID, "I think, therefore I am." In light of the Buddha's teaching, you might say, "I think, therefore I am . . . not here." You are lost in your thinking, so you are really not here. For you to truly be here, thinking has to stop. As you are practicing mindfulness of the breath, the object of your attention is simply the breath. You stop thinking about the past, the future, your pain, your plans, and so forth, and you start to be really here, body and mind united.

Engaged Buddhism

ENGAGED BUDDHISM means engagement not only in social action, but in daily life. The object of this practice is joy in everyday life, which is freedom. We should use our time with a great deal of intelligence, because time is not only money; it is much more precious than that. It is life. A day is twenty-four hours long: do you know how to manage it? You are intelligent and have lots of different talents, but do you know how to manage your days? You must invest yourself 100 percent in organizing the days that are given to you to live. You can do it.

Begin Immediately

THERE IS A LOT that needs to be done in society—work against war, social injustice, and so on. But first we have to come back to our own territory and make sure that peace and harmony are reigning there. Until we do that, we cannot do anything for society. Let us begin immediately.

What I recommend for all of us is to come back to ourselves and take care of the little boy or the little girl who inhabits the depths of our wounded souls. Then we will be calmer, more understanding and loving, and the environment will begin to change. Other people will benefit from our presence, and we will be able to influence them and our society.

141

When We're Hurt

WHEN WE'RE HURT, there are two ways to think. We can think in a way that makes us angrier and want to retaliate. Or we can try to calm ourselves, touch our compassion and understanding, and give ourselves a peaceful mind. This way helps us see that the other person also suffers, and then our anger will dissipate.

142

False Views

PEOPLE NORMALLY CUT reality into compartments, and so are unable to see the interdependence of all phenomena. To see one in all and all in one is to break through the great barrier that narrows one's perception of reality, a barrier that Buddhism calls "the attachment to the false view of the self."

Attachment to the false view of the self means belief in the presence of unchanging entities that exist on their own. To break through this false view is to be liberated from every sort of fear, pain, and anxiety.

143

Everyone Smiles

EVERY TIME WE SMILE, all the generations of our ancestors, our children, and the generations to come—all of whom are within us—smile too. We practice not just for ourselves, but for everyone, and the stream of life continues.

144

Go Back to the Body

BREATHING MINDFULLY takes our mind back to our breath and, if we continue, to our whole body. We go back to our body and reconcile with it. We get to know what's going on in our body, the wrongs we have done, the conflicts we're having, and we'll know what to do and what not to do in order to be on good terms with our body. With mindful breathing, we come to recognize our body as our home. We might say:

> Breathing in, I am aware of my body.
> Breathing out, I smile to my whole body.

145

Conditions Are Favorable

WHEN WE FIRST learn about the teachings on awakening, we think these teachings are new to us. But we already have the seed of awakening within us. Our teacher and our friends on the path only provide the opportunity for us to touch that seed and help it grow.

There are many healthy and wholesome seeds already within our consciousness. With the help of a teacher and a community of practitioners, we can come back to ourselves and touch them. Having access to a teacher and a Sangha are the favorable conditions that allow our seed of awakening to grow.

146

Skillful Dharma

THE DHARMA IS like a powerful lamp, helping people to see deeply into their situation and releasing them from suffering. When a teaching touches real concerns, real suffering, it can help dissolve the obstacles and difficulties that exist in the mind of the listener. When you hear a Dharma talk that is appropriate in these two ways, faithful to both the true teaching and the actual conditions and situation of the listeners, you have the feeling that it is directed to you personally. It is as if the teacher has seen right into your heart, and is speaking to you and you alone. When many people have this feeling, that is the mark of a skillful Dharma talk.

147

Lost in Thought

IN DAILY LIFE, we are often lost in thought. We get lost in regrets about the past, and fears about the future. We get lost in our plans, our anger, and our anxiety. At such moments, we cannot really be here for ourselves. We are not really here for life.

Practice makes it possible for us to be free—to rid ourselves of these obstacles and establish ourselves firmly in the present moment. Practice gives us methods we can use to help us live fully in the present.

148

Fearless Bodhisattvas

BODHISATTVAS ARE those who have penetrated into the reality of no birth and no death. That is why they are fearless, day and night. With that freedom, they can do a lot to help those who are suffering. We can become a buddha only by being in the world of suffering and afflictions. And when we are free, we can ride on the waves of birth and death without fear, helping those who are drowning in the ocean of suffering.

149

When Strong Emotions Arise

WHEN OUR MIND is carried away by strong pain, it helps to go back to our relaxed and peaceful in-breath and out-breath. Eventually, when our painful feeling comes back, we accept it as it is, instead of letting it carry us away and make us more agitated. We don't fight the painful feeling because we know it is part of us, and we don't want to fight ourselves. Pain, irritation, and jealousy are all part of us. As they arise, we can calm them by going back to our in-breath and out-breath. Our peaceful breathing will calm those strong emotions.

———

150

The Arhat

IN OUR SOCIETY, we're inclined to see doing nothing as something negative, even evil. But when we lose ourselves in activities, we diminish our quality of being. We do ourselves a disservice. It's important to preserve ourselves, to maintain our freshness and good humor, our joy and compassion. In Buddhism we cultivate aimlessness, and in fact in Buddhist tradition the ideal person, an arhat or a bodhisattva, is a businessless person—someone with nowhere to go and nothing to do. People should learn how to just be there, doing nothing.

151

Every Breath You Take

SPIRITUAL PRACTICE IS not just sitting and meditating. Practice is looking, thinking, touching, drinking, eating, and talking. Every act, every breath, and every step can be practice and can help us to become more ourselves.

152

The Biggest Obstacle

OFTEN IT IS OUR own knowledge that is the biggest obstacle to us touching suchness. That is why it's very important to learn how to release our own views. Knowledge is the obstacle to knowledge. If you are dogmatic in your way of thinking, it is very difficult to receive new insights, to conceive of new theories and understandings about the world.

———————

153

The Habit of Hurrying

SUPPOSE YOU HAVE the habit of getting into a hurried state while doing such things as shopping or cooking. With mindfulness you recognize that you are rushing around and knocking things over, trying to finish quickly. Then you realize that the energy of being in a hurry has manifested itself. So you breathe in and out mindfully, and you say, "My dear habit energy, here you are again." And as soon as you recognize it, it will lose its strength.

If the energy comes back again, you do this again, and it will continue to lose its strength. You don't have to fight the energy, just recognize it and smile at it. Every time you recognize it, it becomes a little bit weaker, until eventually it can't control you anymore.

154

Look Deeply into Your Perceptions

IN MOST CASES, our perceptions are inaccurate, and we suffer because we are too sure of them. Look at your perceptions and smile to them. Breathe, look deeply into their nature, and you will see that there are many errors in them. For example, that person you are thinking about has no desire to harm you, but you think that he does. It is important not to be a victim of your false perceptions. If you are the victim of your false perceptions, you will suffer a lot. You have to sit down and look at perceptions very calmly. You have to look into the deepest part of their nature in order to detect what is false about them.

Effortless and Enjoyable

MINDFULNESS PRACTICE should be enjoyable, not work or effort. Do you have to make an effort to breathe in? You don't need to make an effort. To breathe in, you just breathe in. Suppose you are with a group of people contemplating a beautiful sunset. Do you have to make an effort to enjoy the beautiful sunset? No, you don't have to make any effort. You just enjoy it.

The same thing is true with your breath. Allow your breath to take place. Become aware of it and enjoy it. Effortlessness. Enjoyment. The same thing is true with walking mindfully. Every step you take is enjoyable. Every step helps you to touch the wonders of life, in yourself and around you. Every step is peace. Every step is joy. That is possible.

156

Good against Evil

DO NOT TURN yourself into a battlefield, with good fighting against evil. Both sides belong to you, the good and the evil. Evil can be transformed into good, and vice versa.

———

157

A Strong Tree in the Storm

PICTURE A TREE in a storm. At the top of the tree, the small branches and leaves are swaying violently in the wind. The tree looks vulnerable, quite fragile—it seems it can break at any time. But if you look at the trunk, you will see that the tree is solid; and if you look down to its root structure, you will know that the tree is deeply and firmly rooted in the soil. The tree is quite strong. It can resist the storm.

We are also a kind of tree. Our trunk, our center, is just below our navel. The zones of our thinking and our emotions are at the levels of our head and chest. When we are taken hold of by a strong emotion, like despair, fear, anger, or jealousy, we should do our best to leave the zone of the storm and go down to the valley to practice breathing in and out. If we stay in the winds of the storm, it may be too dangerous. We can go for refuge into the trunk, breathing in and out, aware of the rising and falling of our abdomen.

158

Come Back to Yourself

MOST PEOPLE ARE afraid to come back to themselves, because that means having to face the pain inside of them. With the practice of mindfulness, the situation changes. We come back to our pain, but now we are well equipped with the energy of mindfulness that has been generated by mindful breathing and by meditation. We use that source of energy to recognize and embrace our pain.

This is very important. If you are unable to take care of yourself, how can you take care of anyone else? How can you take care of the person you love? When you are here for yourself, when you have reestablished some basic order and peace within yourself, then you can take care of the person you love. It could be your son, your daughter, your partner, or your friend. But if you are not able to be here for yourself, it will not be possible for you to be here for them. That's why you must come back to yourself.

159
A Healing Mantra

OUR BODY AND MIND are sustained by the cosmos. The clouds in the sky nourish us; the light of the sun nourishes us. The cosmos offers us vitality and love in every moment. Despite this fact, some people feel isolated and alienated from the world. As a bodhisattva, you can approach such a person, and with this mantra you can open the door of his or her heart to the world and to the love that is always happening: "Dear one, I know that you are suffering a lot. I know this, and I am here for you, just as the trees are here for you and the flowers are here for you." The suffering is there, but something else is also there: the miracle of life. With this mantra, you will help them to realize this and open the door of their closed heart.

The Idea of Birth and Death

IT IS OUR IDEA of birth and death that takes away our peace and happiness in everyday life. And it is meditation that will rid us of the fear that is born from the idea of birth and death. This is the virtue of deep looking in meditation. It helps you to see the heart of reality very deeply. To touch the nature of interbeing is to touch the very nature of no-death and no-birth.

Think Globally

WE MAY FEEL THAT we are incapable of touching the ultimate dimension, but that is not correct. We have done so already. The problem is how to do it more deeply and more frequently. The phrase, "Think globally," for example, is in the direction of touching the ultimate dimension. When we see things globally, we have more wisdom and we feel much better. We are not caught by small situations. When we see globally, we avoid many mistakes, and we have a more profound view of happiness and life.

The Work of Reconciliation

TO RECONCILE MEANS to bring peace and happiness to members of our family, society, and other nations. To promote the work of reconciliation, we have to refrain from aligning ourselves with one party or another so that we understand both. This work takes courage; we may be suppressed or even killed by those we wish to help. After listening to both sides, we can tell each side about the suffering of the other. This alone will bring about greater understanding. Our society needs bodhisattvas who can bridge the huge gaps of misunderstanding between people of different religions, races, and cultures.

163
They Suffer Too

USUALLY WHEN WE SUFFER WE THINK we're the only person who suffers, and that the other person is very happy. But in fact, it's likely that the person who hurts us also has a lot of pain and doesn't know how to handle his strong emotions. Breathing with awareness, we generate our energy of mindfulness, and we can have insight into how to handle our suffering and that of the other person's suffering with compassion.

164

I Ask for Nothing Else

I AM HAPPY in the present moment. I do not ask for anything else. I do not expect any additional happiness or conditions that will bring about more happiness.

———————

Performing Miracles

THE ZEN MASTER Linji (Rinzai) said that the miracle is not to walk on burning charcoal or in the thin air or on the water—the miracle is just to walk on earth. You breathe in. You become aware of the fact that you are alive. You are still alive and you are walking on this beautiful planet. That is already performing a miracle.

166

A Real Friendship

IN PRACTICING mindful breathing, we become a real friend to our body, our emotions, our mind, and our perceptions. Only once we've developed a real friendship with ourselves can we effect some transformation within these different realms. If we want to reconcile with our family or with friends who have hurt us, we have to take care of ourselves first. If we're not capable of listening to ourselves, how can we listen to another person? If we don't know how to recognize our own suffering, it won't be possible to bring peace and harmony into our relationships.

Touching the Ground of Being

WE HAVE TO nourish our insight into impermanence every day. If we do, we will live more deeply, suffer less, and enjoy life much more. Living deeply, we will touch the foundation of reality, nirvana, the world of no-birth and no-death. Touching impermanence deeply, we touch the world beyond permanence and impermanence. We touch the ground of being, and see that what we have called "being" and "nonbeing" are just notions. Nothing is ever lost. Nothing is ever gained.

168

Very Easy

IT ONLY TAKES A few seconds of mindful breathing for your body and mind to begin to come back together again. It is very easy. A child can do it. You just concentrate on your in-breath and on your out-breath. You don't think about anything else. The past, the future, your worries, your anger, and your despair are not there anymore. Only one thing is there: your in-breath and your out-breath. Go ahead and enjoy breathing for twenty minutes, just being here. You are here, and you have nothing to do except enjoy mindful breathing.

———————

The Beauty before You

WHEN YOU ARE looking at a sunset and are in contact with the beauty of nature, practice mindful breathing. Touch deeply the beauty that is before you. I am breathing in—what happiness! I am breathing out—the sunset is lovely! Continue that way for a few minutes.

Getting in touch with the beauty of nature makes life much more beautiful, much more real, and the more mindful and concentrated you are, the more deeply the sunset will reveal itself to you. Your happiness is multiplied by ten, by twenty. Look at a leaf or a flower with mindfulness, listen to the song of a bird, and you will get much more deeply in touch with them. After a minute of this practice, your joy will increase; your breathing will become deeper and more gentle, and this gentleness and depth will influence your body.

———————

The Practice of Nonviolence

BUDDHIST PRACTICE IS based on nonviolence and nondualism. You don't have to struggle with your breath. You don't have to struggle with your body, or with your hate, or with your anger. Treat your in-breath and out-breath tenderly, nonviolently, as you would treat a flower. Later you will be able to do the same thing with your physical body, treating it with gentleness, respect, nonviolence, and tenderness. And when you are dealing with pain, with a moment of irritation, or with a bout of anger, you can learn to treat them in the same way.

Precious Gifts

YOUR MINDFUL BREATH and your smile will bring happiness to you and to those around you. Even if you spend a lot of money on gifts for everyone in your family, nothing you could buy them can give as much true happiness as your gift of awareness, breathing, and smiling, and these precious gifts cost nothing.

Mother and Child

WHEN YOU GROW up, you might believe that you and your mother are two different people. But it's not really so. We're extensions of our mother. We mistakenly believe that we're a different person than our mother. We are a continuation of our mother and father, and our ancestors as well.

Imagine a grain of corn we plant in the soil. Seven days later it sprouts and begins to take the form of a cornstalk. When the stalk has grown high, we won't see the kernel anymore. But the kernel hasn't died. It's still there. Looking deeply, we can still see the kernel in the stalk. The kernel and the stalk are not two different entities; one is the continuation of the other. The stalk is the continuation of the kernel in the direction of the future, and the kernel is the continuation of the stalk in the direction of the past. They are neither the same thing nor two different things. You and your mother are not exactly the same person, but you are not exactly two different people either. This is a very important teaching. No one can be by himself or herself alone. We have to inter-be, connected with everyone and everything else.

173

Formations

WHEN CONDITIONS are sufficient, something manifests. That is what we call a "formation." The flower is a formation, and so are the clouds and the sun. I am a formation, and you are a formation.

174

Free of Our Burdens

REAL HAPPINESS cannot exist when we are not free. Burdened by so many ambitions, we are not able to be free. We are always grasping at something; there are so many things we want to do at the same time, and that is why we do not have the time to live. We think that the burdens we carry are necessary for our happiness, that if they are taken from us we will suffer.

However, if we look more closely, we shall see that the things at which we grasp, the things that keep us constantly busy, are in fact obstacles to our being happy. In letting go of them, we learn that true happiness can only come by way of freedom, an awakened life, and the practice of love and compassion.

———

Let Your Heart Bloom

IN THE SPRINGTIME, thousands of different kinds of flowers bloom. Your heart can also bloom. You can let your heart open up to the world. Love is possible—do not be afraid of it. Love is indispensable to life, and if in the past you have suffered because of love, you can learn how to love again.

———————————

Training for Happiness

LITTLE BY LITTLE you must train yourself for life, for happiness. You probably received a college degree that you spent years working for, and you thought that happiness would be possible after you got it. But that was not true, because after getting the degree and finding a job, you continued to suffer. You have to realize that happiness is not something you find at the end of the road. You have to understand that it is here, now.

The Indivisible Body of Reality

CONTEMPLATION on interdependence is a deep looking into all phenomena in order to pierce through to their real nature, in order to see them as part of the great body of reality, and in order to see that the great body of reality is indivisible. It cannot be cut into pieces that exist separately from each other.

178

The Energy of Mindfulness Will Protect You

THE ENERGY OF MINDFULNESS IS something concrete that can be cultivated. When we practice walking mindfully, our solid, peaceful steps cultivate the energy of mindfulness and bring us back to the present moment. When we sit and follow our breathing, aware of our in- and out-breath, we are cultivating the energy of mindfulness.

When we have a meal in mindfulness, we invest all our being in the present moment, and are aware of our food and of those who are eating with us. We can cultivate the energy of mindfulness while we walk, while we breathe, while we work, while we wash the dishes or wash our clothes. A few days practicing like this can increase the energy of mindfulness in you, and that energy will help you, protect you, and give you courage to go back to yourself, to see and embrace what is there in your territory.

179
A Summary of the Path

MINDFULNESS BRINGS concentration. Concentration brings insight. Insight liberates you from your ignorance, your anger, your craving. When you are free from your afflictions, happiness becomes possible. How can you be happy when you are overloaded with anger, ignorance, and craving? That is why the insight that can liberate you from these afflictions is the key to happiness.

We Are Vast

WE ARE IN the habit of identifying ourselves with our bodies. The idea that we are this body is deeply entrenched in us. But we are not just this body; we are much more than that. The idea that "This body is me and I am this body" is an idea we must get rid of. If we do not, we will suffer a great deal. We are *life,* and life is far vaster than this body, this concept, this mind.

181

A Baby Cries

SUPPOSE A MOTHER is working in the living room and she hears her baby crying. Chances are, she puts down whatever she is doing and goes to her baby's room. She picks up the baby and holds it tenderly in her arms. This is exactly what we can do when the energy of anger comes up. Our anger is our ailing baby. We must embrace it in order to calm it.

The practitioner knows that her anger is not her enemy; her anger is her suffering baby. She must take good care of her baby, using the energy of mindfulness to embrace her anger in the most tender way. She can say: "Breathing in, I know that anger is in me. Breathing out, I am peacefully holding my anger."

———————

182

Inner Conflict

YOU DO NOT have to struggle against a desire. There is no need for a battle within you. Mindfulness is something that embraces and includes things like desire, that recognizes them with great tenderness. Meditation is not about turning yourself into a battlefield where one side fights the other, because the basis of Buddhist meditation is nonduality. The habits of drinking alcohol or getting angry are also you, and therefore you must treat them with great tenderness and nonviolence. The essential point is not to create conflict, a fight, within yourself.

———————

183

Acts of Enlightenment

EVERY TIME WE make a mindful step, we are engaged in an act of enlightenment. We can be enlightened about the fact that we are making a step. Each step can have beauty in it. Washing a dish can be an act of enlightenment. It's delightful to wash the dishes!

184

The River of Feelings

FEELINGS ARE BORN, take shape, last for a few moments, and then disappear. As with the physical form, birth and death of feelings occur in every moment. In meditation, we look mindfully at this river of feelings. We contemplate their arising, their remaining, and their disappearance. We witness their impermanence. When we have an unpleasant feeling, we say to ourselves, "This feeling is in me, it will stay for a while, and then it will disappear because it is impermanent." Just by seeing the impermanence of feelings in this way, we suffer a lot less.

185

The Gap

YOU HAVE A concept of yourself, but have you touched your true self? Look deeply to try to overcome the gap between your concept of reality and reality itself. Meditation helps us remove concepts.

186

The First Noble Truth

THE BUDDHA TOLD us to recognize the First Noble Truth, the truth of suffering, and to look deeply in order to discover the Second Noble Truth, the cause of suffering. That is the only way the Fourth Noble Truth, the path to transform suffering into happiness, can reveal itself. So we have to emphasize the role of suffering. If we are so afraid of suffering, we have no chance.

187

Mindfulness Bell

WHEN I WAS A young monk in Vietnam, each village temple had a big bell, like those in Christian churches in Europe and the United States. Whenever the bell was invited to sound, all the villagers would stop what they were doing and pause for a few moments to breathe in and out in mindfulness. At Plum Village, the community where I live in France, we do the same. Every time we hear the bell, we go back to ourselves and enjoy our breathing. When we breathe in, we silently say, "Listen, listen," and when we breathe out, we say, "This wonderful sound brings me back to my true home."

188

Ideas of Happiness

IF THERE ARE things that are causing you to suffer, you have to know how to let go of them. Happiness can be attained by letting go, including letting go of your ideas about happiness. You imagine that certain conditions are necessary to your happiness, but deep looking will reveal to you that those notions are the very things standing in the way of happiness and are making you suffer.

189

The Apple Tree

HAVE A LOOK AT the apple tree in your yard. Look at it with complete attention. It is truly a miracle. If you notice the apple tree, you will take good care of it, and you too are part of its miraculousness. Even after caring for it for only a week, its leaves are already greener and shinier.

It is exactly the same with the people who are around you. Under the influence of awareness, you become more attentive, understanding, and loving, and your presence not only nourishes you and makes you lovelier, it enhances them as well. Our entire society can be changed by one person's peaceful presence.

A Wonderful Opportunity

HOW CAN WE bring the practice of mindfulness to the widest spectrum of society? How can we give birth to the greatest number of people who are happy and who know how to teach the art of mindful living to others? The number of people who create violence is very great, while the number of people who know how to breathe and create happiness is very small. Every day gives us a wonderful opportunity to be happy ourselves and to become a place of refuge for others.

Love Is Understanding

IN BUDDHISM, it is said that love and compassion are made out of one substance, which is called "understanding." If you understand, you can love. But if understanding is not there, it is impossible for you to accept and love someone. Why did he act that way? Why did he say those things? You should look deeply into these questions, and then you will see the causes of what you are dealing with. With this understanding, you stop blaming and criticizing. Your compassion is born of your understanding of the situation.

192

Return to Wisdom

THE PRACTICES OF mindful walking, mindful sitting, and mindful breathing are our foundation. With our mindful breath and mindful steps, we can produce the energy of mindfulness and return to the awakened wisdom lying in each cell of our body. That energy will embrace us and heal us.

193

Our Inheritance

WE CONTAIN ALL the beautiful qualities and actions of our ancestors, and also all the painful qualities. Knowing this, we can try our best to continue what is good and beautiful in our ancestors, and we will practice to transform the violence and pain passed down to us from so many generations. We know that we practice peace not only for ourselves, but for the benefit of all our ancestors and all our descendants.

194

You Don't Need to Be Someone Else

IF YOU PUT AN aim in front of you, you'll be running all your life, and happiness will never be possible. Happiness is possible only when you stop running, and cherish the present moment and who you are. You don't need to be someone else; you're already a wonder of life.

———

The Fire Consumes the Match

THE TEACHINGS OF IMPERMANENCE and nonself are tools you need to work with, but you should not get caught in them. If you do, impermanence becomes just another concept, and so does nonself. These kinds of concepts are exactly what the Buddha said we should get rid of. He said that nirvana is the complete extinction of concepts, including the concepts of impermanence and nonself. When you want to start a fire, you light a match, and then the fire consumes the match. The teachings of impermanence and nonself are like the match. If you practice with intelligence and succeed in your practice, the match will be consumed and you will be completely free.

196

A Relaxation Practice

WHEN YOU WALK in the hills or in a park or along a riverbank, you can follow your breath with a half-smile blooming on your lips. When you feel tired or irritated, you can lie down with your arms at your sides, allowing all your muscles to relax, maintaining awareness of just your breath and your smile. Relaxing in this way is wonderful, and quite refreshing. You will benefit a lot if you practice it several times a day.

197

Elegant Silence

DURING THE TIME you are practicing mindfulness, you stop talking—not only the talking outside, but the talking inside. The talking inside is the thinking, the mental discourse that goes on and on and on inside. Real silence is the cessation of talking—of both the mouth and of the mind. This is not the kind of silence that oppresses us. It is a very elegant kind of silence, a very powerful kind of silence. It is the silence that heals and nourishes us.

198

Rituals

WHEN WE DO SOMETHING deeply and authentically, it becomes a real ritual. When we pick up a glass of water and drink it, if we're truly concentrated in the act of drinking, it is a ritual. When we walk with all our being, investing 100 percent of ourselves into making a step, mindfulness and concentration become a reality. That step generates the energy of mindfulness and concentration that makes life possible, deep, and real. If we make a second step like that, we maintain that concentration. Walking like that, it looks like we are performing a rite. But in fact we're not performing; we're just living deeply every moment of our life.

———————

199

Driving Lesson

EVEN WHEN YOU ARE driving your car, you can practice. Take advantage of that moment to cultivate mindfulness. In fact, you can practice quite well while you are driving a car. Breathe in and breathe out, and remain aware of everything that goes on inside you when, for example, you come to a red light. You look at the red light and you smile. The red light is not your enemy. It is a friend who is helping you come back to yourself.

———————

You Are a Positive Factor

CULTIVATE SOLIDITY. You are somebody; you are something. You are a positive factor for your family, for society, for the world. You have to recover yourself, to be yourself. You have to become solid again. You can practice solidity in everyday life. Every step, every breath you take should help you become more solid. When you have solidity, freedom is there too.

———

The Work of All Meditators

WE HAVE NO need of a separate self or a separate existence. In fact, nothing can exist by itself. We must inter-be with all things. Look at a flower. It cannot exist by itself. It can only inter-be with the whole cosmos. And that is true for you, too. Getting rid of the concept of self is the work of all meditators, because suffering is born from this concept.

Haunted by the Past

WHEN WE'RE HOLDING the mental formations of despair and suffering, we can look and see that *this* has been born from *that;* suffering is born because we are in touch with an image from the past. The reality is that we are safe, and we have the capacity to enjoy the wonders of life in the present moment. When we recognize that our suffering is based on images instead of current reality, then living happily in the present moment becomes possible right away.

———

Use Time Wisely

HOW DO YOU use your time? You have to make a living, certainly, and you have to support your loved ones. But do you make the effort to arrange your life so you can do some deep looking? That will bring you joy, freedom from fear, and great well-being. You must not let yourself drown in an ocean of fear and suffering. There are among us people who have practiced deep looking, and shared their insight with us. Take advantage of that. Walk on the spiritual path that lets you touch the depths of your being so that you can free yourself from fear, worry, and despair.

Untying the Knots

IN BUDDHIST psychology, the word *samyojana* (Sanskrit) refers to internal formations, fetters, or knots. When someone says something unkind to us, for example, if we do not understand why he said it and we become irritated, a knot will be tied in us. The lack of understanding is the basis for every internal knot. If we practice mindfulness, we can learn the skill of recognizing a knot the moment it is tied in us and finding ways to untie it. Internal formations need our full attention as soon as they form, while they are still loosely tied, so that the work of untying them will be easy.

———————

All Breathe Together

WHEN WE TAKE a breath, we are light, calm, at ease. We breathe in such a way that all generations of ancestors and descendants are breathing with us. Only then are we breathing according to the highest teachings. We just need a little mindfulness, a little concentration, and then we can look deeply and see. At first we can use the method of visualization to see all our ancestors making a step with us. Gradually we don't need to visualize anymore. With each step we take, we see it is the step of all people in the past and future.

206

An Act of Love

A WORK OF ART can help people understand the nature of their suffering, and have insight into how to transform the negative and to develop the positive in themselves. Writing, making a film, creating a work of art can be an act of love. That act of love nourishes you and nourishes others. If you're happy, if you know how to live deeply every moment of your life, then deep understanding, joy, and compassion can come. Your art will reflect this understanding and will share it with others.

Our Collective Wisdom

I BELIEVE THAT in America there are many people who are awakened to the fact that violence cannot remove violence. They realize there is no way to peace: peace itself is the way. Those people must come together and voice their concern strongly, and offer their collective wisdom to the nation.

Dear Buddha

OUR CONCEPTS ABOUT things prevent us from really touching them. We have to destroy our notions if we want to touch the real rose. When we ask, "Dear Buddha, are you a human being?" it means we have a concept about what a human being is. So the Buddha just smiles at us. It is his way of encouraging us to transcend our concepts and touch the real being that he is. A real being is quite different from a concept.

———————

209

The Art of Creating Happiness

WE HAVE TO learn the art of creating happiness. If during your childhood, you saw your parents do things that created happiness in the family, you already know what to do. But many of us didn't have these role models and don't know what to do. The problem is not one of being wrong or right, but one of being more or less skillful. Living together is an art. Even with a lot of goodwill, you can still make the other person very unhappy. The substance of the art of making others happy is mindfulness. When you are mindful, you are more artful.

210

The Real Question

THE QUESTION IS not, how can we obtain love and understanding? The question is whether we have the capacity of generating love and understanding ourselves. If we do, we'll feel wonderful, because these energies satisfy us and the people around us at the same time. That is the love of the Buddha. True love is like that too. Loving one person is really an opportunity to learn to love all people. If you have the capacity to love and to understand, you can do that now; you don't have to wait. When we succeed in this, our worry and fear go away, and we feel wonderful right away.

———————

Healing Wrong Perceptions

ALL THE ENERGIES of anger, hatred, fear, and violence come from wrong perceptions. Wrong perceptions result in a lot of anger, mistrust, suspicion, hate, and terrorism. You cannot remove wrong perceptions through punishment. You have to do it with the tools of deep and compassionate listening and loving speech. The practice of deep and compassionate listening and loving speech can help to build harmony, can remove discrimination, and can bring about the kind of insight that will be liberating to our country and to our people.

The Heart of Life

WHEN YOU LOOK at the nature of things with concentration, you discover that they are all impermanent. Everything is constantly changing. Nothing has a permanent identity. This impermanence is not a negative thing. Impermanence is the very heart of life; it makes life possible. Reject impermanence, and you reject life. It is because of impermanence that everything is possible. Our hope lies in impermanence.

213

Our Baby Buddha

THERE IS A BABY buddha in our store consciousness, and we have to give him or her a chance to be born. When we touch our baby buddha—the seeds of understanding and love that are buried within us—we become filled with *bodhichitta,* the mind of enlightenment, the mind of love. From that moment on, everything we do or say nourishes the baby buddha within us, and we are filled with joy, confidence, and energy. According to Mahayana Buddhism, awakening to our mind of love is the moment the practice begins.

214

I Don't Need These Things

PERHAPS YOU ARE IN contact with too many negative elements. You have looked at, listened to, and touched things that are negative in nature, such as fear and despair. These negative forces are everywhere. When you turn on the television, for instance, you run the risk of ingesting harmful things, such as violence, despair, or fear.

At that moment, you say to yourself with mindfulness, "I don't need these things. I already have suffering, violence, anger, and despair in me. I refuse to watch these programs. I am going to seek out things that are refreshing in nature, healing and helpful things. I will practice walking meditation. I will make contact with the blue sky, with spring, with the song of birds. I will play with my little girl, my little boy. I'll do those kinds of things."

The Ever-Changing Body

WE NEED TO LEARN to see our physical form as a river. Our body is not a static thing—it changes all the time. It is very important to see our physical form as something impermanent, as a river that is constantly changing. Every cell in our body is a drop of water in that river. Birth and death are happening continuously, in every moment of our daily life. We must live every moment with death and life present at the same time. Both death and life are happening at every instant in the river of our physical body. We should train ourselves in this vision of impermanence.

216

Holy Spirit

WHEN THE ENERGY of mindfulness is dwelling in you, Buddha is dwelling in you. The energy of mindfulness is the energy of Buddha. It is the equivalent of the Holy Spirit. Where the Holy Spirit is, there is also understanding, life, healing, and compassion. Where mindfulness is, true life, solidity, freedom, and healing also manifest. We all have the ability to generate this energy of mindfulness. Do walking meditation, breathe mindfully, drink your tea mindfully, and cultivate this energy that dwells in you, that illuminates you, and that makes life possible.

Beyond Labels

As HUMAN BEINGS we're exactly the same. But the many layers of labels prevent other people from seeing you as a human being. Thinking of yourself as or calling yourself a "Buddhist" can be a disadvantage, because if you wear the title "Buddhist" this may be an obstacle that prevents others from discovering the human being in you. The same is true whether you are Christian, Jewish, or Muslim. This can be an important part of your identity, but it is not the whole of who you are. People are caught in these notions and images, and they cannot recognize each other as human beings. The practice of peeling away all the labels so that the human being can be revealed is truly a practice for peace.

218

Forgetfulness

MOST PEOPLE ARE FORGETFUL; they are not really there a lot of the time. Their mind is caught in their worries, their fears, their anger, and their regrets, and they are not mindful of being there. That state of being is called "forgetfulness"—you are there, but you are not there. You are caught in the past or in the future. You are not there in the present moment, living your life deeply. That is forgetfulness.

The opposite of forgetfulness is mindfulness. Mindfulness is when you are truly there, mind and body together. You breathe in and out mindfully, you bring your mind back to your body, and you are there. When your mind is there with your body, you are established in the present moment. Then you can recognize the many conditions of happiness that are in you and around you, and happiness just comes naturally.

What the Buddha Really Said

THE BUDDHA did not say, "You don't exist." He only said, "You are without self." Your nature is nonself. We suffer, because we think he's saying we don't exist. From one extreme we fall into another extreme, but both extremes are just our notions. We never experience reality. We only have these notions, and we suffer because of them.

What Channel Will You Turn On?

EVEN THOUGH LIFE is hard, even though it is sometimes difficult to smile, we have to try. Recently, one friend asked me, "How can I force myself to smile when I am filled with sorrow? It isn't natural." I told her she must be able to smile to her sorrow, because we are more than our sorrow.

A human being is like a television set with millions of channels. If we turn the Buddha on, we are the Buddha. If we turn sorrow on, we are sorrow. If we turn a smile on, we really are the smile. We can't let just one channel dominate us. We have the seeds of everything in us, and we have to take the situation in hand to recover our own sovereignty.

Embrace the Presence of the Other

PLEASE TRY THIS practice. You can practice mindfulness of the breath for a minute or walk mindfully toward the person you love most in the world. Then you are truly here, truly present. You open your mouth and you utter the magic words of the mantra: "Dear one, I am really here for you." You embrace the presence of the other with the mindfulness that is within you.

A Very Naive Idea

MANY PEOPLE ASPIRE to go to a place where pain and suffering do not exist, a place where there is only happiness. This is a rather dangerous idea, for compassion is not possible without pain and suffering. It is only when we enter into contact with suffering that understanding and compassion can be born. Without suffering, we do not have the opportunity to cultivate compassion and understanding; and without understanding, there can be no true love. So we should not imagine a place where there is no suffering, where there is only happiness. That would be a very naive idea.

Benefit from the Positive Elements

IF THE PRESENCE of the other is refreshing and healing to you, keep hold of this presence and nourish yourself with it. If there are negative things around you, you can always find something that is healthy, refreshing, and healing, and with your mindfulness you can recognize its presence in your life.

You need to recognize that these kinds of positive elements exist and that you can benefit from their refreshing and helpful presence. If you are facing a sunset, a marvelous spectacle, give yourself a chance to be in touch with it. Give yourself five minutes, breathing deeply, and you will be truly there. Touch the beauty of nature in a deep way. That will do your body and mind a great deal of good.

The Importance of Resting

RESTING IS THE first part of Buddhist meditation. Our mind as well as our body needs to rest. The problem is that not many of us know how to allow our body and mind to rest. We are always struggling; struggling has become a kind of habit. We cannot resist being active, struggling all the time. It is very important to realize that we have the habit energy of struggling. We have to be able to recognize a habit when it manifests itself because if we know how to recognize our habit, it will lose its energy and will not be able to push us anymore.

———

Precious Hours

ON THE WOODEN board outside of the meditation hall in Zen monasteries, there is a four-line inscription. The last line is, "Don't waste your life." Our life is made of days and hours, and each hour is precious.

———————

Manifest Miracles

CONCENTRATION IS the practice of happiness. There is no happiness without concentration. When you eat an orange, try to practice concentration. Eat it in such a way that pleasure, joy, and happiness are possible the whole time. You look at the orange, and breathe in such a way that it reveals itself as the miracle it is. An orange is nothing less than a miracle. It is just like you—you are also a miracle of life. You are a manifest miracle.

227

Vipassana

THE PALI WORD *vipassana* (Sanskrit: *vipashyana*) means "to go deeply into that object to observe it." When we are fully aware of an object and observing it deeply the boundary between the subject who observes and the object being observed gradually dissolves, and the subject and object become one. This is the essence of meditation. Only when we penetrate an object and become one with it can we understand. It is not enough to stand outside and observe an object.

———

Overthrow "Self"

WHEN SHAKYAMUNI BUDDHA put forth the notion of "no self," he upset many concepts about life and the universe. He blasted our most firm and widespread conviction—that of a permanent self. Those who understand "no self" know that its function is to overthrow "self," not to replace it with a new concept of reality. The notion of "no self" is a method, not a goal. If it becomes a concept, it must be destroyed along with all other concepts.

Jesus and Buddha

SOMEONE ONCE asked me, "If the Buddha and Jesus Christ were to meet today, what would they have to say to each other?" And my answer is, the Buddha and Jesus Christ are already meeting every day, everywhere. Because Buddhists are the continuation of the Buddha, and Christians are the continuation of Jesus, and they are meeting today everywhere. We should help make their meeting successful.

For the Person You Love

HAVE YOU OFFERED your presence to the person you love? Are you so busy that you cannot be there for that person? If you are a father or a mother or a partner, generate your own presence, because that is the most precious gift you can offer.

———————

231

Learning from the Past

THE BUDDHA SAID that we should not be afraid of the past; but he did warn us not to lose ourselves in it, either. We should not feed our regret or pain over the past, and we should not get carried away by the past. We do need to study and understand the past, however, because by looking deeply into the past we learn a lot of things that can benefit the present and the future. The past is an object of our study, of our meditation, but the way to study it or meditate on it is by remaining anchored in the present moment.

232

Touch the Earth

WALKING IS A FORM of touching the earth. We touch the earth with our feet, and we heal the earth, we heal ourselves, and we heal humankind. Whenever you have an extra five, ten, or fifteen minutes, enjoy walking. With every step it's possible to bring healing and nourishment to our body and to our mind. Every step taken in mindfulness and freedom can help us heal and transform, and the world will be healed and transformed together with us.

The Sun Always Shines

WHEN IT IS raining, we think that there is no sunshine. But if we fly high in an airplane and go through the clouds, we rediscover the sunshine again. We see that the sunshine is always there. In a time of anger or despair, our love is also still there. Our capacity to communicate, to forgive, to be compassionate is still there.

You have to believe this. We are more than our anger; we are more than our suffering. We must recognize that we do have within us the capacity to love, to understand, to be compassionate. If you know this, then when it rains you won't be desperate. You know that the rain is there, but the sunshine is still there somewhere. Soon the rain will stop, and the sun will shine again. Have hope. If you can remind yourself that the positive elements are still present within you and the other person, you will know that it is possible to break through, so that the best things in both of you can come up and manifest again.

234

The Foundation of Change

THE PRACTICE OF the Dharma cannot be individual anymore. It should be a collective practice. Teachers should practice with other teachers and students; psychotherapists should practice with their clients and other therapists. Filmmakers should make films that inspire awakening. Journalists should write articles that help people to wake up. Everyone has to do the work of promoting awakening. Awakening is the foundation of every kind of change.

Nothing Is Created or Lost

IF WE LOOK deeply into the nature of reality, we will see that nothing is created or lost. As the Buddhist text called the *Prajnaparamita* says, there is neither birth nor death. Birth is a concept, death is too, and neither of these concepts is applicable to reality. We must make the effort to look into this truth deeply to confirm it for ourselves.

236

Is This Accurate?

THE BUDDHA SAID that our perceptions are very often false, and since error is there, suffering is there also. We must pay very close attention to this. We have to learn how to look at our perceptions without getting caught by them. We must always ask ourselves the question, "Is my perception accurate?" Just asking that question is a big help.

The Second Arrow

THE BUDDHA SPEAKS ABOUT the "second arrow." When an arrow strikes you, you feel pain. If a second arrow comes and strikes you in the same spot, the pain will be ten times worse.

The Buddha advised that when you have some pain in your body or your mind, breathe in and out and recognize the significance of that pain, but don't exaggerate its importance. If you stop to worry, to be fearful, to protest, to be angry about the pain, then you magnify the pain ten times or more. Your worry is the second arrow. You should protect yourself and not allow the second arrow to come, because the second arrow comes from you.

238

Nothing to Regret

FEAR OF THE unexpected leads many people to live a constricted and anxious life. No one can know in advance the misfortunes that may happen to us and our loved ones, but if we learn to live in an awakened way, living deeply every moment of our life, treating those who are close to us with gentleness and understanding, then we will have nothing to regret when something happens to us or to them. Living in the present moment, we are able to be in touch with life's wonderful, refreshing, and health-giving phenomena, which allow us to heal the wounds in ourselves. Every day we become more wonderful, fresh, and healthy.

———————

Peace Permeates

IF THROUGH mindfulness of the breath you generate harmony, depth, and calm, these will penetrate into your body and mind. In fact, whatever happens in the mind affects the body, and vice versa. If you generate peacefulness in your breathing, that peacefulness permeates your body and your state of mind.

240

Rest Naturally

SUPPOSE SOMEONE is holding a pebble and throws it in the air, and the pebble begins to fall down into a river. After the pebble touches the surface of the water, it allows itself to sink slowly into the river. It will reach the bed of the river without any effort. Once the pebble is at the bottom of the river, it continues to rest. It allows the water to pass by. I think the pebble reaches the bed of the river by the shortest path because it allows itself to fall without making any effort.

During our sitting meditation we can allow ourselves to rest like a pebble. We can allow ourselves to sink naturally without effort to the position of sitting, the position of resting.

———————

What Are You Doing?

ONE DAY AS I WALKED through the kitchen, I saw someone cleaning vegetables and I asked, "What are you doing?" I was playing the role of a spiritual friend. Even though it was obvious that they were washing vegetables, I asked the question to wake the person up to how happy they could be, just washing the vegetables. If we aren't doing something with joy, that moment is wasted.

The Right Path

HAPPINESS MEANS feeling you are on the right path every moment. You don't need to arrive at the end of the path in order to be happy. The right path refers to the very concrete ways you live your life in every moment. In Buddhism, we speak of the Noble Eightfold Path: Right View, Right Thought, Right Speech, Right Action, Right Livelihood, Right Effort, Right Mindfulness, and Right Concentration. It's possible for us to live the Noble Eightfold Path every moment of our daily lives. That not only makes us happy, it makes people around us happy. If you practice the path, you become very pleasant, very fresh, and very compassionate.

———————

A Declaration of Love

WHAT IS LOVING? It is recognizing the presence of the other with your love. This is not a theory; it is a practice. Whether the object of your love is your heart, your in-breath, your physical body, or your baby, whether it is your son, your daughter, or your partner, your declaration of love is always the same. It is: "Dear one, I am here for you."

244

Look a Little Deeper

WE ALL KNOW that understanding and compassion can relieve suffering. This is not just a platitude; where there is understanding and compassion, there's relief and help for ourselves and others. Our practice is to keep that understanding and compassion alive. As busy as we are, when we take time to look a little bit more deeply, we can always find more understanding and compassion to offer.

The Sangha Body of Peace

THE MOMENT WHEN you sit down and begin to breathe in, calming your mind and your body, peace has become a reality. That kind of breathing is like praying. When there is the element of peace in you, you can connect with other people, and you can help others to be peaceful like you. Together you become a body of peace, the Sangha body of peace.

246

One Contains All

WHEN YOU TOUCH one thing with deep awareness, you touch everything. The same is true of time. When you touch one moment with deep awareness, you touch all moments. According to the *Avatamsaka Sutra,* "The one contains the all." If you live one moment deeply, that moment contains all the past and all the future in it.

———————

247

Nirvana Is Now

NIRVANA IS THE ultimate dimension of life, a state of coolness, peace, and joy. It is not a state to be attained after you die. You can touch nirvana right now by breathing, walking, and drinking your tea in mindfulness. You have been "nirvanized" since the very nonbeginning. Everything and everyone is dwelling in nirvana.

248

Mother Earth

THE EARTH HAS been there for a long time. She is mother to all of us. She knows everything. The Buddha asked the Earth to be his witness by touching her with his hand when he had some doubt and fear before his awakening. The Earth appeared to him as a beautiful mother. In her arms she carried flowers and fruit, birds and butterflies, and many different animals, and offered them to the Buddha. The Buddha's doubts and fears instantly disappeared.

Whenever you feel unhappy, come to the Earth and ask for her help. Touch her deeply, the way the Buddha did. Suddenly, you too will see the Earth with all her flowers and fruit, trees and birds, animals, and all the living beings that she has produced. All these things she offers to you.

249

Space Is Freedom

WHEN YOU ARRANGE flowers, it is good to leave space around each flower so it can reveal itself in its full beauty and freshness. You don't need a lot of flowers—two or three are enough.

We human beings also need space to be happy. We practice stopping and calming in order to offer space to ourselves, inside and outside, and also to those we love. We need to let go of our projects, preoccupations, worries, and regrets, and create space around us. Space is freedom.

———

250

Touched by Her Light

SUPPOSE THERE IS someone who lives very mindfully, dwelling in concentration. She comes home, goes out, stands, sits, speaks, chops vegetables, washes pots, carries out all the activities of daily life in mindfulness and concentration. In all her actions of body, speech, and mind, she shines the light of mindfulness. When others encounter her they are able to get in touch with that mindfulness, and they are influenced by it. Touched by the light of her mindfulness, the seed of mindfulness in their own consciousness begins to sprout, and naturally they also begin to cultivate mindfulness in their activities as she does.

———

251

Many Wonders

LIFE IS FILLED with suffering, but it is also filled with many wonders, such as the blue sky, the sunshine, and the eyes of a baby. To suffer is not enough. We must also be in touch with the wonders of life. They are within us and all around us, everywhere, in every moment.

252

Natural Parenting

IF PARENTS PRACTICE mindfulness and compassion in their daily lives, the children will naturally learn from them. We can't tell a child to do something if we don't do it ourselves. From time to time, parents might discuss mindfulness and compassion with their children, and express their wish that their children will continue living in mindfulness and with more compassion.

When you use loving speech, you can water the good seeds in your children and inspire them to do as you have done. You don't have to punish or blame them. With right speech and by following your own practice, your children will see, and they will follow you.

253

With Deep Insight

MINDFULNESS HELPS us to recognize the many conditions of happiness that are available in the here and the now. Concentration helps us to get in touch more deeply with these conditions. With enough mindfulness and concentration, insight is born. With deep insight, we are free of wrong perceptions and we can maintain our freedom for a long time. With deep insight, we don't get angry anymore, we don't despair anymore, and we can enjoy each moment of life.

254

In the Presence of God

THE PRINCIPLE OF the practice is simple: to bring our mind back to our body, to produce our true presence, and to become fully alive. Everything is happening under the light of mindfulness. In the Jewish and Christian traditions, we say, "We're doing everything in the presence of God." That's another way of expressing the same reality.

Buddha Is Always Possible

THE BUDDHA SAID that every one of us can become a buddha like him. If we have love, understanding, and peace, if we can transform our anger, our jealousy, then we can become a buddha like him. And in the cosmos there are many other buddhas. Wherever there are human beings, there is the possibility of a buddha, or many buddhas, manifesting.

———

Mind Creates Everything

OUR MIND CREATES everything. The majestic mountaintop, brilliant with snow, is you yourself when you contemplate it. Its existence depends on your awareness. When you close your eyes, as long as your mind is present, the mountain is there. Sitting in meditation, with several sense-windows closed, you feel the presence of the whole universe. Why? Because the mind is there. If your eyes are closed, it is so that you can see better. The sights and sounds of the world are not your enemies. Your enemy is forgetfulness, the absence of mindfulness.

———

A Kind of Death

WHEN WE STUDY Buddhism, we look for a teacher and we believe that teacher has wisdom. We have to believe that the teacher is holy and that other people are ordinary in order for us to be able to follow that teacher. The teacher puts on the robe of holiness, and we believe he immediately becomes holy. That is the place that kills us. It's a kind of death when we run away from the ordinary toward what we think is holy. Then we run away from ourselves.

258

Which World Do We Choose?

THERE ARE TWO worlds, and we can choose which one we want to live in: the world of awakening or the world of ignorance. If we haven't yet stopped our ideas, we live in ignorance. Ignorance doesn't have a dwelling place. It has no beginning and no end. If we live in the world of awakening, we will be happy in our daily life. Why don't we do it?

The Greatest Practice

NONFEAR IS THE greatest practice in Buddhism. To free ourselves from all fear, we must touch the ground of our being and train ourselves to look directly into the light of compassion. The *Heart Sutra* describes how the bodhisattva Avalokiteshvara, because he is able to look deeply into the nonself nature of the five aggregates (*skandhas*), discovers the nature of emptiness and immediately overcomes all afflictions. From this he receives the energy of nonfear, which is why he is able to help so many others. Once we have seen that our afflictions are none other than enlightenment, we too can ride joyfully on the waves of birth and death.

Indescribable Freedom

CONCEPTS AND IDEAS are incapable of expressing reality as it is. Nirvana, the ultimate reality, cannot be described, because it is free of all concepts and ideas. Nirvana is the extinction of all concepts. It is total freedom. Nirvana, the ultimate reality, or God, is of the nature of no-birth and no-death.

Our Natural Tendency

THERE'S A NATURAL tendency in us to seek pleasure and to avoid suffering. We have to instruct our mind that suffering can sometimes be very helpful. We can even speak of the "goodness of suffering." Thanks to suffering, we begin to understand. And because we understand, we can accept, we can love. Without understanding and love, there cannot be any happiness. So suffering has to do with happiness. We should not be afraid of suffering. We should be able to hold our suffering and look deeply into it, hold it tenderly, and learn from it.

———————

262

A Moment of Infinity

TOUCHING THE present moment does not mean getting rid of the past or the future. As you touch the present moment, you realize that the present is made of the past and is creating the future. Touching the present, you touch the past and the future at the same time. You touch the infinity of time, the ultimate dimension of reality.

Watering Their Flowers

IF WE PRACTICE the art of mindful living together, we see that the other person, like us, has both flowers and compost inside, and we accept this. Our practice is to water the flowerness in her, and not bring her more garbage. We avoid blaming and arguing. When we try to grow flowers, if the flowers do not grow well, we do not blame or argue with them. We ask ourselves what we can do to help them grow more beautifully.

To help a flower grow well, we must understand her nature. How much water does she need? How much sunshine? We look deeply into ourselves to see our true nature, and we look into the other person to see her nature.

Compassionate Listening

COMPASSIONATE listening is crucial. We listen with the willingness to relieve the suffering of the other person, not to judge or argue with her. We listen with all our attention. Even if we hear something that is not true, we continue to listen deeply so the other person can express her pain and release the tensions within herself. If we reply to her or correct her, the practice will not bear fruit. If we need to tell the other person that her perception was not correct, we can do that a few days later, privately and calmly.

———————

You Have Already Arrived

ALL WE HAVE TO do is be ourselves, fully and authentically. We don't have to run after anything. We already contain the whole cosmos. We simply return to ourselves through mindfulness, and touch the peace and joy that are already present within us and all around us.

I have arrived. I am already home. There is nothing to do. Aimlessness, nonattainment, is a wonderful practice.

266

Releasing Tension

WHEN WE COME home to the present moment, we become aware of our body, and all of our tension is released. Everyone can practice paying attention to their breath, perhaps repeating these words, "Breathing in, I am aware of my body. Breathing out, I release the tension in my body." You don't need to be a Buddhist to practice this. You can sit in whatever position you feel comfortable, and practice releasing the tension and tightness in your body. One or two minutes of practice can already make a big difference.

———————

267

How Strange

AT THE MOMENT of his awakening at the foot of the Bodhi tree, the Buddha declared, "How strange! All beings possess the capacity to be awakened, to understand, to love, to be free, yet they allow themselves to be carried away on the ocean of suffering." He saw that, day and night, we're seeking what is already there within us.

No Provenance

ALL THINGS HAVE NO provenance. They have not come from anywhere, because they are free from the ideas of being and nonbeing. They do not have to be born. They cannot be grasped by our notions, or discriminated by our mental categories. They have come from nowhere; they will go nowhere. There is no author or creator.

That is the true nature of reality. We can only touch and experience things when we are free from the concepts of birth and death, creator and created. All things have no provenance; therefore they have no birth. Because they have no birth, extinction cannot be found either. That is the way things are.

269

Every Thought Becomes Sacred

EACH THOUGHT, each action in the sunlight of awareness becomes sacred. In this light, no boundary exists between the sacred and the profane.

Love Your Own Heart

WHAT IS LOVE? Love is treating your beating heart with a great deal of tenderness, with understanding, love, and compassion. If you cannot treat your own heart this way, how can you treat your partner with understanding and love?

271

Our Common Well-Being

WE HAVE TO wake up to the fact that everything is connected to everything else. Our safety and well-being cannot be individual matters anymore. If others are unsafe, there is no way that we can be safe. Taking care of other people's safety is taking care of our own safety. To take care of their well-being is to take care of our own well-being. It is the mind of discrimination and separation that is at the foundation of all violence and hate.

Which Seeds Will We Cultivate?

ACCORDING TO the Buddha, the birth of a human being is not a beginning but a continuation, and when we're born, all the different kinds of seeds—seeds of goodness, of cruelty, of awakening—are already inside us. Whether the goodness or cruelty in us is revealed depends on what seeds we cultivate, our actions, and our way of life.

Long Live Impermanence!

IF YOU SUFFER, it's not because things are impermanent. It's because you believe things are permanent. When a flower dies, you don't suffer much, because you understand that flowers are impermanent. But you cannot accept the impermanence of your beloved one, and you suffer deeply when she passes away. If you look deeply into impermanence, you will do your best to make her happy right now. Aware of impermanence, you become positive, loving, and wise.

Impermanence is good news. Without impermanence, nothing would be possible. With impermanence, every door is open for change. Instead of complaining, we should say, "Long live impermanence!" Impermanence is an instrument for our liberation.

Nondualism

THE MODE OF being that is expressed by the Buddha is at the heart of reality. It's not the notion we usually construct for ourselves. Our notion of being is dualistic. We think of it as the opposite of the notion of nonbeing. The reality of being that the Buddha tries to convey is not the opposite of nonbeing. He's using language differently. When he says "self," it's not the opposite of anything. The Buddha is very aware that self is made of nonself elements. That is our true self.

A Very Challenging Practice

WE WOULD ALL like to have the time to sit and appreciate the stillness that comes from doing nothing. But if we were given the time, would we be able to be still and quiet? That is the problem with many of us. We complain that we don't have the time to rest, to enjoy being here. But we are used to always doing something. We have no capacity to rest and do nothing. Even if we have a rare moment of quiet at our desks, we talk on the phone or browse the Internet. We are workaholics. We always need to be doing something, or we think we will die. That is why learning how to be right where we are without doing anything is a very important practice, as well as a very challenging one.

276

Resurrection

SOME PEOPLE LIVE as though they are already dead. There are people moving around us who are consumed by their past, terrified of their future, and stuck in their anger and jealousy. They are not alive; they are just walking corpses. If you look around yourself with mindfulness, you will see people going around like zombies. Have a great deal of compassion for the people around you who are living like this. They do not know that life is accessible only in the here and now.

We must practice resurrection, and this is an everyday practice. With an in-breath, you bring your mind back to your body. In this way you become alive in the here and now. Joy, peace, and happiness are possible. You have an appointment with life, an appointment that is in the here and now.

Simply Illuminate

THERE IS NO NEED TO MANIPULATE the breath. Breath is a natural thing, like air, like light; we should leave breath as it is and not interfere with it. What we are doing is simply lighting up the lamp of awareness to illuminate our breathing. We generate the energy of mindfulness to illuminate everything that is happening in the present moment.

Beyond Forms

THE BEST WAY to practice is according to the spirit of nonpractice, not clinging to forms. Suppose you practice sitting meditation very well. People look at you and see that you are a diligent practitioner. You sit perfectly, and you begin to feel a little proud. While others sleep late and do not come to the meditation hall on time, you are there sitting beautifully.

With that kind of feeling in you, the happiness that results from your practice will be limited. But if you realize that you are practicing for everyone, even if the whole community is sleeping and you are the only one sitting, your sitting will benefit everyone and your happiness will be boundless. We should practice meditation this way—without form, in the spirit of nonpractice.

279

The Secret to Happiness

HAPPINESS IS a function of compassion. If you do not have compassion in your heart, you do not have any happiness.

———————

Being Peace

THERE ARE MANY of us who are eager to work for peace, but we don't have peace within. Angrily we shout for peace. And angrily we shout at the people who, like us, are also for peace; even people and groups dedicated to peacemaking sometimes fight among themselves. If there is no peace in our heart, there can be no harmony among the peace workers. And if there is no harmony, there is no hope. If we're divided, if we're in despair, we can't serve; we can't do anything.

Peace must begin with ourselves: with the practice of sitting quietly, walking mindfully, taking care of our body, releasing the tension in our body and in our feelings. That is why the practice of being peace is at the foundation of the practice of doing peace. Being peace comes first. Doing peace is something that comes from that foundation.

Loving Words

EVERY TIME THE other person does something well, we should congratulate him or her to show our approval. This is especially true with children. We have to strengthen the self-esteem of our children. We have to appreciate and congratulate every good thing they say and do in order to help our children grow.

We don't take things for granted. If the other person manifests some talent or capacity to love and create happiness, we must be aware of it and express our appreciation. This is the way to water the seeds of happiness. We should avoid saying destructive things like, "I doubt that you can do this." Instead, we say, "This is difficult, darling, but I have faith you can do it." This kind of talk makes the other person stronger.

282

Insecurity

WE ALL FEEL insecure. We don't know what the future holds: accidents happen, a loved one may suddenly be struck by an incurable disease and die, we are not sure if we'll be alive tomorrow. This is all part of impermanence, and this feeling of insecurity makes us suffer.

How can we face this feeling? What is our practice? I think living deeply in the present moment is what we have to learn and practice so we can face this feeling of insecurity. We have to handle the present moment well. We live deeply in the present moment so that in the future we will have no regrets. We are aware that both we and the person in front of us are alive. We cherish the moment and do whatever we can to make life meaningful and to make him happy in this moment.

———

Rest on Your Cushion

WHEN I SIT on my meditation cushion, I consider it to be something very pleasant. I don't struggle at all on my cushion. I allow myself to be, to rest. I don't make any effort, and that is why I do not have any trouble while sitting. While sitting I do not struggle, and that is why all my muscles are relaxed. If you struggle during your sitting meditation, you will very soon have pain in your shoulders and back and things like that. But if you allow yourself to be rested on your cushion, you can sit for a very long time, and each minute is light, refreshing, nourishing, and healing.

284

Transforming Your Past

IF YOU BEHAVED badly in the past, if you have been destructive, you can do something about it. By touching the present deeply, you can transform the past. The wounds and injuries of the past are still there—they are within your reach. All you have to do is come back to the present moment, and you will recognize the wounds and injuries that you have caused in the past and those that other people have caused you.

You should be here for these wounds and injuries. You can say to them, "I am here for you," with your mindful breathing, your deep looking, and your determination not to do the same thing again. Then transformation is possible.

———

285

A Raft to the Other Shore

THE BUDDHA SAID to consider his teaching to be a raft helping you to the other shore. What you need is a raft to cross the river in order to go to the other shore. You don't need a raft to worship, to carry on your shoulders, and to make you proud that you are possessing the truth.

A Simple Question

THIS MORNING I picked a tender green leaf off the ground. Is this leaf in my mind or outside of it? What a question! It's a very simple question, but very difficult to answer.

The notion of "outside" and "inside" cannot be applied to reality. We tend to think of the mind as "in here" and the world as "out there," the mind as subjective and the world, the body, as objective. The Buddha taught that mind and object of mind do not exist separately; they inter-are. Without this, the other cannot be. There is no perceiver without the perceived. Object and subject manifest together.

Start with a Single Breath

ANYONE CAN succeed in the practice of a single conscious breath. If we continue to breathe consciously for ten breaths, without our mind going astray, then we have taken a valuable step on the path of practice. If we can practice conscious breathing for ten minutes, an important change will take place in us.

———————

No Inferiority Complex

MANY OF US go around all the time feeling that we are as small as a grain of sand. We may feel that our one small human life doesn't have very much meaning. We struggle to get through life, and at the end of our life we feel that we have accomplished very little.

This is a kind of inferiority complex many people suffer from. If we see reality only in terms of the historical dimension, it may seem to us as if there is little one ordinary human being can do. But if we get in touch with the ultimate dimension of reality, we know that we are just like the Buddha. We share in the Buddha's nature—we *are* Buddha nature. When we are able to see beyond the limitations of perceived time and space, beyond our own notions of inferiority and powerlessness, we find we have great stores of spiritual energy to share with the world.

Trust in the Sangha

WE NEED TO TRUST in the Sangha, the community of practitioners. It is made up of people who are practicing mindfulness, who generate the collective energy of mindfulness, every moment of the day. You should put your trust in that energy. Every time you take a step or breathe mindfully, you generate the energy of the Buddha. This protects you and heals you. But if you are a beginner, the energy you generate may not be strong enough to handle the suffering in you. You need to combine your energy with the energy of the group. In that way, healing and transformation can take place very quickly.

Our Desire for Permanence

WHEN WE LOOK deeply into our fear, we see the desire for permanence. We're afraid of change. Our anger, our fear, our despair are born from our wrong perceptions, from our notions of being and nonbeing, coming and going, rising and falling. If we practice looking deeply, we find out that these notions cannot be applied to reality. We can touch our true nature, we can touch the ultimate dimension, and this brings about nonfear. When we trust that insight of no birth and no death, joy becomes possible every moment of our life.

Meditation Is Not Solemn

MEDITATION IS TO be aware of what is going on—in our body, in our feelings, in our mind, and in the world. Each day nine thousand children die of hunger. The superpowers have more than enough nuclear warheads to destroy our planet many times. Yet the sunrise is beautiful, and the rose that bloomed this morning along the wall is a miracle. Life is both dreadful and wonderful. To practice meditation is to be in touch with both aspects. Please do not think we must be solemn in order to meditate. In fact, to meditate well, we have to smile a lot.

Every Step a Prayer

IN THE SPIRIT OF Buddhism, anything you do that is accompanied by mindfulness, concentration, and insight can be considered a prayer. When you drink your tea in forgetfulness, you are not truly alive because you're not there, you're not mindful, and you're not concentrated. That moment is not a moment of practice.

When you hold your cup and drink your tea in mindfulness and concentration, it's like you're performing a sacred ritual, and that is a prayer. When you walk, if you enjoy every step, if every step nourishes and transforms you, then every step is a prayer. When you sit in solidity and freedom, when you breathe in and out in mindfulness, when you touch the wonders of life, that is meditation and that is also prayer.

293
Sexuality

THE HUMAN BODY is beautiful, and sexuality can be something beautiful and spiritual. Without sexuality, a buddha cannot come into the world. We can't separate mind from body; our body is as sacred as our mind. That's why when we look at the body as an item of consumption, an object of desire, we haven't truly seen the body. Our body should be treated with utmost respect. When we touch someone else's body, we touch their mind and their soul.

More Time for What Is Important

TIME IS VERY precious: every minute, every hour counts. We don't want to throw time away. We want to make good use of the minutes and the hours we have left. When we focus our attention in the here and now and live simply, we have more time to do the things we think are important. We don't waste our energy in thinking, in worrying, in running after fame, power, and wealth.

———

295
A Rain of Wisdom

WHEN YOU LISTEN to a talk or read a book about the Dharma, it's not for the purpose of getting notions and ideas. In fact, it's for releasing notions and ideas. You don't replace your old notions and ideas with new ones. The talk or the writings should be like the rain that can touch the seed of wisdom and freedom within you. That's why we have to learn how to listen. We listen or read not to receive more notions and concepts, but in order to get free from all notions and concepts. What's important is not that you remember what was said, but that you are free.

296

Infinite Interaction

TO BE IMPERMANENT means not to be the same thing in two consecutive moments; there is always something coming in and something going out, input and output. Everything is interacting with every other thing, and therefore touching impermanence is also touching interbeing. Interbeing means you don't have a separate existence, you inter-are with everything else.

———

297

Have a Lazy Day

TRY TO SPEND a day doing nothing; we call that a lazy day. Although for many of us who are used to running around from this to that, a lazy day is actually very hard work! It's not so easy to just be. If you can be happy, relaxed, and smiling when you're not doing something, you're quite strong. Doing nothing brings about quality of being, which is very important. So doing nothing is actually something. Please write that down and display it in your home: *Doing nothing is something.*

298

Spiritual Research

SPIRITUAL PRACTITIONERS don't use sophisticated research instruments. They use their inner wisdom, their luminosity. Once we get rid of grasping, of notions and concepts, once we get rid of our fear and our anger, then we have a very bright instrument with which to experience reality as it is, reality free from all notions, such as birth and death, being and nonbeing, coming and going, the same or different. The practice of mindfulness, concentration, and insight can purify our mind and make it into a powerful instrument with which we can look deeply into the nature of reality.

The Definition of Hell

TO ME, THE definition of hell is simple: it is a place where there is no understanding and no compassion. We have all been to hell. We are acquainted with hell's heat, and we know that hell is in need of compassion. If there is compassion, then hell ceases to be hell.

You can generate this compassion yourself. If you can bring a little compassion to this place, a little bit of understanding, it ceases to be hell. You can be the bodhisattva who does this. Your practice consists in generating compassion and understanding and bringing them to hell. Hell is here, all around us. Hell is in us, like a seed. We need to cultivate the positive within us so we can generate the energy of understanding and compassion and transform hell. Hell is a matter of everyday life, like the Kingdom of God. The choice is yours.

300

Two Kinds of Knots

THERE ARE TWO kinds of knots. One knot is our notions and ideas. Everyone has notions and ideas, and we are attached to them; we are not free, so we have no chance to touch the truth in life. The second knot is our afflictions like fear, anger, discrimination, despair, and arrogance. All these things should be removed in order for us to be free.

The Best Thing to Cultivate

MINDFULNESS IS A PRACTICE to enjoy, not to bring about more hardship in our life. The practice is not hard labor; it's a matter of enjoyment. And enjoyment can become a habit. Some of us only have the habit of suffering. Others among us have cultivated the habit of smiling and being happy. The capacity to be happy is the best thing we can cultivate. So please enjoy walking, enjoy sitting. We enjoy sitting and walking for ourselves, for our ancestors, for our parents, our friends, our beloved ones, and for our so-called enemies.

302

No Ideas

WHEN WE LOOK deeply, we see that all our ideas about our body and about our mind are inaccurate. We have to practice no ideas. "No ideas" doesn't mean to stop thinking and perceiving. Rather we have to go beyond ideas and not get caught in perceptions of permanence and of a separate self.

When we can stop every idea in our mind, that is awakening. "No ideas" can also be translated as "emptiness." When we can see the emptiness of each thing, then we get to the place where there is no idea. And awakening doesn't lie far away, it lies within our perception. There's a Chinese saying: "If you stop the idea in your mind, that is the Bodhi tree."

303
The Milky Way

THE MILKY WAY doesn't say, "I am the Milky Way." It *is* the Milky Way. In reality, the wonderful reality is life. We are that wonderful reality. We ourselves are present here with a clear light that can illuminate and reflect everything as it is.

———

Reminders

IN PLUM VILLAGE, every time the phone rings everyone practices mindful breathing in and out. So the bell is a friend, an invention of practitioners to help us.

If you work on a computer, you might get so carried away by your work that you forget that you're alive. So you may like to program your computer so that every quarter of an hour it offers the sound of the bell, enabling you to go back to yourself, to smile and breathe in and out before you continue work. Many of our friends have done that. A bell reminding you to come back to yourself and enjoy breathing is a wonderful way to take a break.

305

Sit with Your Fear

THE BUDDHA advises us not to try to run away from our fear, but to bring up our fear and have a deep look into it. Most of us try to cover up our fear. Most of us are afraid of looking directly at our fear. Instead of trying to distract yourself from this fear or ignore it, the Buddha proposed that you bring the seed of fear up, and recognize that it's there and embrace it with your mindfulness.

Sitting with your fear, instead of trying to push it away or bury it, can transform it. This is true of all of your fears, both small ones and big ones. You don't have to try and convince yourself not to be afraid. You don't have to try to fight or overcome your fear. Over time you'll find that when your fear comes up again, it will be a little bit weaker.

The Best Moment of Your Life

IF SOMEONE WERE to ask us, "Has the best moment of your life arrived yet?" we may say that it will come very soon. But if we continue to live in the same way, it may never arrive. We have to transform this moment into the most wonderful moment, and we can do that by stopping—stopping running to the future, stopping worrying about the past, stopping accumulating so much. You are a free person; you are alive. Open your eyes and enjoy the sunshine, the beautiful sky, and the wonderful children all around you. Breathing in and out consciously helps you become your best—calm, fresh, solid, clear, and free, able to enjoy the present moment as the best moment of your life.

The Three Realms

IF WE LET A DESIRE rise within us, that is the desire realm. If we give rise to anger, that is the form realm. If we give rise to a moment of doubt, that is the formless realm. The three realms are made of craving, anger, and ignorance. When we have compassion, love, and understanding, then we're no longer in the three realms, we're in the Pure Land. No gas or plane ticket is needed to take us there.

308

Sit like a Mountain

SITTING QUIETLY, just breathing in and out, we develop strength, concentration, and clarity. So sit like a mountain. No wind can blow the mountain down.

How to Listen to the Dharma

LISTENING TO A Dharma talk is a practice. When you are hearing a teaching, you should sit in such a way that peace, relaxation, and ease are possible. Don't struggle. Just open yourself to allow the Dharma to penetrate you, the way rain penetrates soil. You should not use intellect to receive the Dharma. The intellect can be like a sheet of plastic covering the earth, preventing the rain of Dharma from penetrating the ground of your being. The ground of your being contains lots of seeds, and it needs the rain to penetrate deeply into it. So do not use only the intellect. Do not compare and discriminate. Just open up to the Dharma rain, and let it penetrate you.

310

Here to Love

IN ORDER TO LOVE, you must be here. That is certain. Fortunately, being here is not a difficult thing to accomplish. It is enough to breathe and let go of thinking or planning. Just come back to yourself, concentrate on your breath, and smile. You are here, body and mind together. You are here, alive, completely alive. That is a miracle.

_____

To Be a Source of Comfort

THOSE WHO WORK with the dying need to practice solidity and nonfear. Others need our stability and nonfear in order to be able to die peacefully. If we know how to touch the ultimate dimension of reality, if we know the reality of no birth and no death, we can transcend all fear. Then, when we are sitting with a dying person, we can be a source of comfort and inspiration to them.

None Other Than Enlightenment

OUR AFFLICTIONS ARE none other than enlighten-ment. We can ride the waves of birth and death in peace. With the boat of compassion, we can travel on the ocean of delusion with a smile of nonfear. In the light of inter-being, we see the flower in the garbage and the garbage in the flower. It is on the very ground of suffering, the ground of afflictions, that we can contemplate enlighten-ment and well-being. It is exactly in the muddy water that the lotus grows and blooms.

Beginning the Day

EVERY twenty-four-hour day is a tremendous gift to us. So we all should learn to live in a way that makes joy and happiness possible. We can do this. I begin my day by making an offering of incense while following my breath. I think to myself that this day is a day to live fully, and I make the vow to live each moment of it in a way that is beautiful, solid, and free. This only takes me three or four minutes, but it gives me a great deal of pleasure.

You can do the same thing when you wake up. Breathe in and tell yourself that a new day has been offered to you, and you have to be here to live it.

314

Melt the Ice of Knowledge

IN BUDDHISM, knowledge is regarded as an obstacle to understanding, like a block of ice that obstructs water from flowing. It is said that if we take one thing to be the truth and cling to it, even if truth itself comes in person and knocks at our door, we won't open it. For things to reveal themselves to us, we need to be ready to abandon our views about them.

———

Contemplating Body in the Body

THE BUDDHA HAD a special way to help us understand the object of our perception. He said that in order to understand, you have to be one with what you want to understand. In the *Satipatthana Sutta,* the basic manual on meditation from the time of the Buddha, it is recorded, "The practitioner will have to contemplate body in the body, feelings in the feelings, mind in the mind, objects of mind in the objects of mind."

The words are clear. The repetition "body in the body" is not just to underline the importance of it. "Contemplating body in the body" means that you do not stand outside of something to contemplate it. You must be one with it, with no distinction between the contemplator and the contemplated. "Contemplating body in the body" means that you should not look on your body as the object of your contemplation. You have to be one with it. The message is clear. *Nonduality* is the key word for Buddhist meditation.

316

The Smile of Nonfear

BECAUSE BODHISATTVAS are free from fear, they can help many people. Nonfear is the greatest gift we can offer to those we love. Nothing is more precious. But we cannot offer that gift unless we ourselves have it. If we have practiced and have touched the ultimate dimension of reality, we too can smile the bodhisattvas' smile of nonfear. Like them, we don't need to run away from our afflictions. We don't need to go somewhere else to attain enlightenment. We see that afflictions and enlightenment are one. When we have a deluded mind, we see only afflictions. But when we have a true mind, the afflictions are no longer there. There is only enlightenment. We are no longer afraid of birth and death because we have touched the nature of interbeing.

Don't Water the Seeds of Suffering

WHEN WE ARE irritated and we say something unkind to our child, we water the seeds of suffering in him. When he reacts, he waters the seeds of suffering in us. Living this way escalates and strengthens the suffering. In mindfulness, calmly breathing in and out, we can practice looking deeply at the types of suffering we have in ourselves. When we do so, we also begin to understand our ancestors, our culture, and our society. The moment we see this, we can go back and serve our people with loving kindness and compassion, and without blame. Because of our insight, we are capable of practicing real peace and reconciliation.

318

True Generosity

TRUE GENEROSITY is not a trade or a bargaining strategy. In true giving, there is no thought of giver and recipient. This is called "the emptiness of giving," in which there is no perception of separation between the one who gives and the one who receives.

This is the practice of generosity given in the spirit of wisdom, with the understanding of interbeing. You offer help as naturally as you breathe. You don't see yourself as the giver and the other person as the recipient of your generosity, who is now beholden to you and must be suitably grateful, respond to your demands, and so on. You don't give so you can make the other person your ally. When you see that people need help, you offer and share what you have with no strings attached and no thought of reward.

———

319

Action Is Being

LOOK AT THE TREE in the front yard. The tree doesn't seem to be doing anything. It stands there, vigorous, fresh, and beautiful, and everyone profits from it. That's the miracle of being. If a tree were less than a tree, all of us would be in trouble. But if a tree is just a real tree, then there's hope and joy. That's why if you can be yourself, this is already action. Action is based on nonaction; action is being.

———————

320

Dry Bones

INSIGHT CAN'T BE found in sutras, commentaries, or Dharma talks. Liberation and awakened understanding can't be found by devoting ourselves to the study of the Buddhist scriptures. This is like hoping to find fresh water in dry bones. Returning to the present moment, using our clear mind that exists right here and now, we can be in touch with liberation and enlightenment, as well as with the Buddha and all his disciples as living realities right in this moment.

321

Be There for Breakfast

WHEN YOU EAT your breakfast, even if it is just a small bite early in the morning, eat in such a way that freedom is possible. While eating breakfast, don't think of the future, of what you are going to do. Your practice is to simply eat breakfast. Your breakfast is there for you; you have to be there for your breakfast. You can chew each morsel of food with joy and freedom.

Concentrated Pleasure

TRUE PLEASURE IS EXPERIENCED in concentration. When you walk and you are 100 percent concentrated, the joy you get from the steps you are taking is much greater than the joy you would get without concentration. You have to invest 100 percent of your body and mind in the act of walking. Then you will experience that being alive and taking steps on this planet are miraculous things.

323

The Kingdom of God Is Right Here

THE KINGDOM OF GOD is not a mere notion. It is a reality that can be touched in everyday life. The Kingdom of God is now or never, and we all have the ability to touch it—not only with our minds, but with our feet. The energy of mindfulness helps you in this. With one mindful step, you touch the Kingdom of God.

324

A Dangerous Notion

THE NOTION OF death, of nothingness, is very dangerous. It makes people suffer a lot. In Buddhist teaching, nothingness is only a concept, and it is never applicable to reality.

———————

325

Don't Try So Hard

THERE ARE PEOPLE who do a lot, but who also cause a lot of trouble. The more they try to help, the more trouble they create, even if they have the best intentions. They're not peaceful, they're not happy. It's better not to try so hard, but just to "be." Then peace and compassion are possible in every moment. On that foundation, everything you say or do can only be helpful.

———

326

Equanimity

TRUE LOVE DOES not just choose one person. When true love is there, you shine like a lamp. You don't just shine on one person in the room. That light you emit is for everyone in the room. If you really have love in you, everyone around you will benefit—not only humans, but animals, plants, and minerals. Love, true love, is that. True love is equanimity.

———————

Cherish the Time You're Given

WHEN WE WALK for the sake of walking, when we sit for the sake of sitting, when we drink tea for the sake of drinking tea, we don't do it for something or someone else. These things can be very enjoyable.

That is the practice of aimlessness. While you do that, you heal yourself and you help heal the world. Awakening means to see this truth—that you want to know how to enjoy, how to live deeply, in a very simple way. You don't want to waste your time anymore. Cherish the time that you are given.

———

328

Anywhere You Go

SUPPOSE YOU ARE standing in line waiting to copy something at work, or waiting to talk with a colleague. You may be out at lunch or waiting in line to get coffee or tea. You can still practice mindful breathing, and focus on enjoying yourself and the presence of people around you. Meditation can be very informal.

329

A New Holiday

WE HAVE holidays for so many important occasions—Christmas, the New Year, Mother's Day, Father's Day, even Earth Day. Why not celebrate a day when we can live happily in the present moment all day long? I would like to declare today "Today's Day," a day dedicated to touching the earth, touching the sky, touching the trees, and touching the peace that is available in the present moment.

———————

A Loving Community of Two

WHEN YOU FIRST fall in love and you feel attached to the other person, that is not yet real love. Real love means loving-kindness and compassion, the kind of love that does not have any conditions. You form a community of two in order to practice love—taking care of each other, helping your partner blossom, and making happiness something real in that small community. Through your love for each other, through learning the art of making one person happy, you learn to express your love for the whole of humanity and all beings.

331

The Four Noble Truths

I THINK WHEN people listen to the teachings of the Four Noble Truths, they hear the words *ill-being* and *suffering,* and they think that Buddhism is only about suffering. They don't know that the Third Noble Truth is about happiness, the opposite of suffering. There is suffering, and there's a path leading to suffering. But there is also the cessation of suffering, which means happiness, and there is a path leading to happiness.

Maybe it would be good to put the Third and Fourth Noble Truths first. The first truth would be happiness, and the second truth would be the path leading to happiness. Then the third truth would be suffering, and the fourth would be the causes of suffering.

———————

332

Reflections in the Heart

EVERYTHING—THE TREES, the wind, the birds, the mountains, everything inside us and around us—wants to reflect itself in us. We don't have to go anywhere to obtain the truth. We only need to be still, and things will reveal themselves in the still water of our heart.

———————

333

Recognizing Negative Energy

NEGATIVE HABIT energy always tries to emerge, but if you are mindful, you recognize it. Mindfulness helps us to recognize the habits transmitted by our ancestors and parents, or learned during our childhood. Often, just recognizing these habits will make them lose their hold on you.

334

The True Teacher in You

THE CAPACITY TO be enlightened isn't something that someone else can offer to you. A teacher can only help you to remove the nonenlightened elements in you so that enlightenment can be revealed. If you have confidence that beauty, goodness, and the true teacher are in you, and if you take refuge in them, you will practice in a way that reveals these qualities more clearly each day.

335

Dependent Coarising

THE BUDDHA TAUGHT that "This is like this, because that is like that." You see? Because you smile, I am happy. This is like this, therefore that is like that. And that is like that, because this is like this. This is called "dependent coarising."

336

Suddenly Alive Again

MANY PEOPLE ARE lost in worries about the future, and regrets about the past. They are caught up in their projects and their fantasies, and their minds are not connected to their bodies. If the body is not united with the mind, we are not really alive. Mindful walking and mindful breathing help bring the mind back to the body, so we can be truly present in the here and now and become truly alive. Practicing mindfulness can be a kind of resurrection; suddenly, you become alive again.

337

Aches and Tensions

WHEN I BREATHE IN, I generate the energy of mindfulness. With this energy, I recognize my body's aches and tensions, I begin to embrace my body tenderly, and allow any tension to be released. Many of us accumulate a lot of tension and pressure in our bodies, working them too hard. It's time to come home to our body. This is possible anytime, whether we are sitting, lying, standing, or walking.

———————

338
The Art of Stopping

WE PRACTICE TO have enough strength to confront problems effectively. To do this, we must be calm, fresh, and solid. That is why we need to practice the art of stopping. When we learn to stop, we become calmer, and our mind becomes clearer, like clear water after the particles of mud have settled.

339

Seated on a Lotus Flower

THE BUDDHA IS often portrayed as sitting on a lotus flower, very fresh, very stable. If we're capable of sitting in the here and the now, anywhere we sit becomes a lotus flower.

Hugging Meditation

HUGGING MEDITATION is a combination of East and West. According to the practice, you have to really hug the person you are hugging. You have to make him or her very real in your arms. You don't do it just for the sake of appearance, patting him on the back two or three times to pretend you are there. You are really there, so you do not have to do that. You breathe consciously while hugging, and you hug with all your body, spirit, and heart. "Breathing in, I know my dear one is in my arms, alive. Breathing out, he is so precious to me." While you hold him and breathe in and out three times, the person in your arms becomes real, and you become very real also.

341

The Paradise of Forms and Colors

YOU CAN LIVE in such a way that you are in the Kingdom of God every moment. This is not just a wish, and it is not a promise of some future happiness. This is a reality. An hour of mindfulness practice, even fifteen minutes, is already enough to prove to you that mindfulness is possible, that real life is possible. A beautiful sunset is something that exists; the song of a bird and the blue sky also exist. The paradise of forms and colors is always accessible.

———————

342

A Mistaken Notion

MANY PEOPLE THINK that in order to avoid suffering, they have to give up joy, and they call this "transcending joy and suffering." This is not correct. If you recognize and accept your pain without running away from it, you will discover that although pain exists, joy also exists. Without experiencing relative joy, you will not know what to do when you are face-to-face with absolute joy. Don't get caught in theories or ideas, such as saying that suffering is an illusion, or that we have to "transcend" both suffering and joy. Just stay in touch with what is actually going on, and you will touch the true nature of suffering *and* the true nature of joy.

343

You Contain Multitudes

EVERY ONE OF US is a miraculous flower in the garden of humanity. If you look deeply into yourself, you will see that you possess everything. As the poet Walt Whitman said, "I am large, I contain multitudes." The one contains all—that is the insight of Buddhism. If you practice deep looking, you will discover this truth, the mystery of inter-being: the one contains all.

344

To Cherish Your Beloved

WHEN WE KNOW that the person we love is impermanent, we will cherish our beloved all the more. Impermanence teaches us to respect and value every moment and
all the precious things around us and inside of us. When
we practice mindfulness of impermanence, we become
fresher and more loving.

———————

345
Eating in Silence

EATING IN SILENCE, even for a few minutes, is a very important practice. It takes away all the distractions that can keep us from really being in touch with the food. Our mindfulness may be fragile, and it may be too difficult to carry on a conversation and really honor the food at the same time. So for the first five or ten minutes, it is wonderful to eat in silence.

What Separates Us

WE ARE SEPARATED BY LABELS, by words like *Israeli, Palestinian, Buddhist, Jew,* and *Muslim.* When we hear one of these words it evokes an image, and we immediately feel alienated from the other group or person. We've set up many habitual ways of thinking that separate us from each other, and we make each other suffer.

People are caught in these notions and images, and they cannot recognize each other as human beings. The practice of peeling away all the labels so that the human being can be revealed is truly a practice for peace.

347

The Bodhisattvas Will Smile Back

WHEN WE PRACTICE walking meditation for even a few days, we will undergo a deep transformation, and we will learn how to enjoy peace in each moment of our life. We will smile, and countless bodhisattvas throughout the cosmos will smile back at us because our peace is so deep. Everything we think, feel, and do has an effect on our ancestors and all future generations, and reverberates throughout the universe.

348

Not a Philosophy

MANY TEACHERS and philosophers such as Heraclitus and Confucius have spoken about impermanence. But the impermanence spoken of by the Buddha is not a philosophy. It is an instrument for your practice of looking deeply. Use the key of impermanence to unlock the door of reality—the nature of interbeing, of no-self, of emptiness. That is why you should not look on impermanence as a notion, a theory, or a philosophy, but as an instrument offered by the Buddha so that we can practice looking deeply and discover the true nature of reality.

———————

349

You Nourished Each Other

IT IS IMPORTANT to remember that you were nourished before you were born. If you look deeply, you will see that at the same time you also nourished your mother. Because of your presence in her body, her body changed and grew. She may have been more tired or not felt well, but at the same time, she may have smiled more and loved life even more.

———————

350

Goodness Is Always in You

BEAUTY AND GOODNESS are always there in each of us. This is the basic teaching of the Buddha. A true teacher, a true spiritual partner, is one who encourages you to look deeply in yourself for the beauty and love you are seeking. The true teacher is someone who helps you discover the teacher in yourself.

351

They Will Reveal Their Splendor

IF WE PRACTICE mindfulness, we get in touch with the refreshing and joyful aspects of life in us and around us, the things we are not able to touch when we live in forgetfulness. Mindfulness makes things like our eyes, our heart, the beautiful moon, and the trees deeper and more beautiful. If we touch these wonderful things with mindfulness, they will reveal their full splendor.

———

352

No Enemy, No Savior

IF WE'RE FREE of the notions of self and nonself, then we won't be afraid of the words *self* and *nonself.* But if we see the self as our enemy and think that nonself is our savior, we are caught. We're trying to push away one thing and embrace another. When we realize that to take care of the self is to take care of what is not self, we are free, and we don't have to push away either.

353

Why Hurry to the Grave?

THERE IS NO NEED for us to struggle to arrive somewhere else. We know that our final destination is the cem-
etery. Why are we in a hurry to get there? Why not step in
the direction of life, which is in the present moment?

———————

354

The Energy of Love

THE TEACHING OF the Buddha aims at helping us to generate the energy of love and understanding. If we can produce that energy, it will first of all help us to satisfy our need to be loved. And then, with that capacity of love and understanding, we can embrace the people who are with us now. We can make them happy while we are happy ourselves.

———————

355

Your Suffering Needs You

GO BACK AND take care of yourself. Your body needs you, your feelings need you, your perceptions need you. Your suffering needs you to acknowledge it. Go home and be there for all these things.

———————————

356

The Buddha's Highest Teaching

EXISTENCE AND nonexistence are just concepts. There is only manifestation and nonmanifestation, which depend on our perception. If you have perception that is deep enough, a deep insight into life, then you are free from all these concepts such as being and nonbeing, birth and death. This is the highest level of the Buddha's teaching. You are looking for relief for your pain, but the greatest relief that you can ever obtain comes from touching the nature of no-birth and no-death.

357

The Simple Act of Walking

WALKING IS AS simple as putting one foot in front of the other. But we often find it difficult or tedious. We drive a few blocks rather than walk in order to "save time." When we understand the interconnectedness of our body and our mind, the simple act of walking like the Buddha can feel supremely easy and pleasurable.

So Many Reasons to Be Happy

WE HAVE SO MANY reasons to be happy. The earth is filled with love for us, and patience. Whenever she sees us suffering, she will protect us. With the earth as a refuge, we need not be afraid of anything, even dying. Walking mindfully on the earth, we are nourished by the trees, the bushes, the flowers, and the sunshine. Touching the earth is a very deep practice that can restore our peace and our joy.

359

A Family Meal

IT IS IMPORTANT for each family to have at least one meal together every day. This meal should be an occasion to practice mindfulness, and to be aware of how fortunate we are to be together. After we sit down, we look at each person and, breathing in and out, smile to him or her for a few seconds. This practice can produce a miracle. It can make you real, and it can make the others at the table real also.

———————

360

Don't Be a Prisoner

THE BUDDHA handed us an instrument to remove notions and concepts, and touch reality directly. If you continue to cling, even to Buddhist notions and concepts, you miss the opportunity. You are carrying the raft on your shoulders. Do not be a prisoner of any doctrine or ideology, even Buddhist ones.

361

Offering Flowers to the Buddha

WHEN A FLOWER dies, we don't cry. We know it is impermanent. If we practice awareness of the nature of impermanence, we will suffer less and enjoy life more. If we know things are impermanent, we will cherish them in the present moment. Impermanence is not negative. Some Buddhists think we should not enjoy anything, because everything is impermanent. They think that emancipation is to get rid of everything and not enjoy anything. But when we offer flowers to the Buddha, I believe the Buddha sees the beauty of the flowers and deeply appreciates them.

362

Big Brother, Big Sister

THE GOOD MUST take care of the evil as a big brother takes care of his little brother, or as a big sister takes care of her little sister—with a great deal of tenderness, in a spirit of nonduality. Knowing that, there is a lot of peace in you already.

———————

363

Why Wait to Be Happy?

MANY PEOPLE IN our society are not happy, even though the conditions for their happiness already exist. Their habit energy is always pushing them ahead, preventing them from being happy in the here and now. But with a little bit of training, we can all learn to recognize this energy every time it comes up. Why wait to be happy?

———————

364

The Essence of Buddhist Meditation

THOSE WHO HAVE practiced Buddhist meditation know that meditating is above all being present: to yourself, to those you love, to life.

365

This Is the Revolution

WE HAVE TO wake up! We have to make it possible for the moment of awareness to manifest. This is the practice that will save us—this is the revolution.

———————————

SOURCES

1. *A Rose for Your Pocket*, p. 24.   2. *Shambhala Sun*, March 2006.   3. *The Sun My Heart*, p. 39–40.   4. *Keeping the Peace*, p. 17.   5. *Shambhala Sun*, March 2006.   6. Ibid., March 2010.   7. *You Are Here*, p. 27.   8. Ibid., p. 86.   9. *Touching Peace*, p. 35–36.   10. *Reconciliation*, p. 32.

11. *You Are Here*, p. 107–8.   12. *Touching Peace*, p. 117.   13. *Understanding Our Mind*, p. 245–46.   14. *You Are Here*, p. 25.   15. *Calming the Fearful Mind*, p. 66.   16. *You Are Here*, p. 3.   17. *Creating True Peace*, p. 39–40.   18. *Cultivating the Mind of Love*, p. 111.   19. *You Are Here*, p. 4.   20. *Reconciliation*, p. 46–47.

21. Ibid., p. 41.   22. Ibid., p. 2.   23. *Shambhala Sun*, July 2004.   24. *Reconciliation*, p. 94.   25. *You Are Here*, p. 30–31.   26. *Shambhala Sun*, March 2006.   27. *Calming the Fearful Mind*, p. 8.   28. *Understanding Our Mind*, p. 45.   29. *Creating True Peace*, p. 5.   30. *Understanding Our Mind*, p. 242–43.

31. *Shambhala Sun*, March 2006.   32. *Our Appointment with Life*, p. 44.   33. *Peaceful Action, Open Heart*, p. 18.   34. *The Heart of the Buddha's Teaching*, p. 3.   35. *Reconciliation*, p. 23–24.   36. *Touching Peace*, p. 36–37.   37. *Shambhala Sun*, March 2006.   38. *Keeping the Peace*, p. 20.   39. *Reconciliation*, p. 105.   40. *Answers from the Heart*, p. 75.

41. *Understanding Our Mind*, p. 242–43.   42. *Reconciliation*, p. 48–50.   43. *You Are Here*, p. 38.   44. *Reconciliation*, p. 28.   45. *The Miracle of Mindfulness*, p. 15.   46. *Creating True Peace*, p. 88–89.   47. *Reconciliation*, p. 117.   48. *Keeping the Peace*, p. 16.   49. *Reconciliation*, p. 20.   50. *Being Peace*, p. 41.

51. *Zen Keys*, p. 28–29.   52. *Reconciliation*, p. 65.   53. *The Heart of the Buddha's Teaching*, p. 133.   54. *The Miracle of Mindfulness*, p. 24.   55. Ibid., p. 12.   56. *You Are Here*, p. 5.   57. *Answers from the Heart*, p. 18–19.   58. Ibid., p. 76.   59. *Touching Peace*, p. 43.   60. *Reconciliation*, p. 15.

61. *You Are Here*, p. 109.   62. Ibid., p. 99.   63. Ibid., p. 18–19.   64. Ibid., p. 9.   65. Ibid., p. 12–13.   66. *Being Peace*, p. 13.   67. *Reconciliation*, p. 58.   68. *The Sun My Heart*, p. 128.   69. *Buddha Mind, Buddha Body*, p. 2.   70. *Reconciliation*, p. 39.

71. Ibid., p. 25.   72. Ibid., p. 70.   73. Ibid., p. 35.   74. Ibid., p. 24.   75. *You Are Here*, p. 40–41   76. *Creating True Peace*, p. 38.   77. *You Are Here*, p. 119.   78. *Reconciliation*, p. 3   79. Ibid., p. 45–46.   80. *Touching Peace*, p. 102.

81. *Reconciliation*, p. 55–56.   82. *Touching Peace*, p. 101–2.   83. *The Blooming of a Lotus*, p. 52.   84. Ibid., p. 6–7.   85. *Shambhala Sun*, July 2010.   86. *Reconciliation*, p. 47.   87. *You Are Here*, p. 40.   88. *Touching Peace*, p. 117.   89. *You Are Here*, p. 88–89.   90. *The Blooming of a Lotus*, p. 58.

91. *Shambhala Sun*, March 2006.   92. *Reconciliation*, p.

100.   93. *Answers from the Heart,* p. 97.   94. *The Miracle of Mindfulness,* p. 49.   95. *Cultivating the Mind of Love,* p. 56.   96. *Reconciliation,* p. 4.   97. *A Rose for Your Pocket,* p. 24.   98. *You Are Here,* p. 80–81.   99. *Shambhala Sun,* March 2006.   100. *The Heart of the Buddha's Teaching,* p. 153.

101. *The Miracle of Mindfulness,* p. 36.   102. *You Are Here,* p. 75–76.   103. *Answers from the Heart,* p. 113–14.   104. *Reconciliation,* p. 20.   105. *Shambhala Sun,* March 2006.   106. *The Heart of the Buddha's Teaching,* p. 154.   107. *You Are Here,* p. 30–31.   108. *Cultivating the Mind of Love,* p. 50.   109. *Shambhala Sun,* May 2008.   110. *The Heart of the Buddha's Teaching,* p. 146.

111. *You Are Here,* p. 51.   112. Ibid., p. 69.   113. *Touching Peace,* p. 8.   114. *You Are Here,* p. 32.   115. Ibid., p. 31.   116. *Touching Peace,* p. 91.   117. Ibid., p. 18–19.   118. Ibid., p. 52–53.   119. *You Are Here,* p. 43.   120. *The Miracle of Mindfulness,* p. 37–38.

121. Ibid., p. 46.   122. *The Heart of the Buddha's Teaching,* p. 148.   123. *A Rose for Your Pocket,* p. 52–53.   124. *Reconciliation,* p. 42.   125. *Shambhala Sun,* May 2008.   126. *You Are Here,* p. 3–5.   127. Ibid., p. 70.   128. Ibid., p. 6–7.   129. Ibid., p. 39–40.   130. *Touching Peace,* p. 78–79.

131. *Our Appointment with Life,* p. 46.   132. *The Heart of the Buddha's Teaching,* p. 136.   133. *You Are Here,* p. 35.   134. *Reconciliation,* p. 69.   135. *Shambhala Sun,* May 2008.   136. *Reconciliation,* p.

62.   137. Ibid., p. 30–31.   138. *You Are Here*, p. 34.   139.
Ibid., p. 81.   140. Ibid., p. 65–66.

141. *Reconciliation*, p. 37.   142. *A Rose for Your Pocket*, p.
43.   143. Ibid.   144. *Reconciliation*, p. 37–38.   145. *Understanding Our Mind*, p. 35.   146. *Peaceful Action, Open Heart*,
p. 64.   147. *You Are Here*, p. 26.   148. *Understanding Our
Mind*, p. 242–43.   149. *Reconciliation*, p. 36–37.   150. *Answers from the Heart*, p. 14.

151. *Shambhala Sun*, May 2008.   152. *Buddha Mind,
Buddha Body*, p. 48.   153. *Answers from the Heart*, p. 19–
20.   154. *You Are Here*, p. 29.   155. *Shambhala Sun*, March
2010.   156. *You Are Here*, p. 3–5.   157. *Touching Peace*, p.
16–17.   158. *You Are Here*, p. 58.   159. Ibid., p. 94.   160.
Ibid., p. 85–86.

161. *Touching Peace*, p. 121.   162. Ibid., p. 88–89.   163.
Reconciliation, p. 37.   164. *The Heart of the Buddha's Teaching*, p. 154.   165. *Shambhala Sun*, March 2006.   166. *Reconciliation*, p. 36.   167. *The Heart of the Buddha's Teaching*,
p. 133.   168. *You Are Here*, p. 33.   169. Ibid., p. 6.   170.
Ibid., p. 2–3.

171. *The Sun My Heart*, p. 20.   172. *Reconciliation*, p.
19–20.   173. *You Are Here*, p. 30.   174. *The Blooming
of a Lotus*, p. 66.   175. *You Are Here*, p. 91.   176. Ibid., p.
80–81.   177. *The Miracle of Mindfulness*, p. 46–47.   178.
Shambhala Sun, March 2006.   179. Ibid., July 2010.   180.
You Are Here, p. 127.

181. *Keeping the Peace*, p. 24.   182. *You Are Here*, p.

70.   183. *Reconciliation,* p. 41.   184. *You Are Here,* p. 28.   185. *The Heart of the Buddha's Teaching,* p. 130.   186. *Shambhala Sun,* July 2010.   187. *Touching Peace,* p. 1.   188. *You Are Here,* p. 73.   189. *The Sun My Heart,* p. 39–41.   190. *The Heart of the Buddha's Teaching,* p. 155.

191. *Creating True Peace,* p. 17–18.   192. *Reconciliation* p. 2–3   193. *Creating True Peace* p. 17–18   194. *Answers from the Heart,* p. 17.   195. *You Are Here,* p. 114.   196. *The Sun My Heart,* p. 20.   197. *Shambhala Sun,* March 2010.   198. Ibid., May 2008.   199. *You Are Here,* p. 21.   200. Ibid., p. 43.

201. Ibid., p. 106.   202. *Reconciliation,* p. 52.   203. *You Are Here,* p. 112.   204. *Touching Peace,* p. 48.   205. *Reconciliation,* p. 22–23. 206. *Answers from the Heart,* p. 114.   207. *Shambhala Sun,* July 2004.   208. *The Heart of the Buddha's Teaching,* p. 129–30.   209. *Shambhala Sun,* March 2006.   210. *Answers from the Heart,* p. 55.

211. *Shambhala Sun,* July 2004.   212. *You Are Here,* p. 103–4.   213. *Cultivating the Mind of Love,* p. 6.   214. *You Are Here,* p. 19–20.   215. Ibid., p. 27.   216. Ibid., p. 8.   217. *Answers from the Heart,* p. 123.   218. *Shambhala Sun,* March 2010.   219. *Cultivating the Mind of Love,* p. 50.   220. *Being Peace,* p. 15–16.

221. *You Are Here,* p. 17.   222. Ibid., p. 10.   223. Ibid., p. 19–20.   224. *Shambhala Sun,* March 2006.   225. *Being Peace,* p. 40.   226. *You Are Here,* p. 79–80.   227. *Transformation and Healing,* p. 8.   228. *The Sun My Heart,* p.

51.   229. *Answers from the Heart*, p. 85–86.   230. *You Are Here*, p. 18–19.

231. Ibid., p. 46.   232. *Buddha Mind, Buddha Body*, p. 115.   233. *Anger*, p. 90.   234. *Answers from the Heart*, p. 99–100.   235. *You Are Here*, p. 83.   236. Ibid., p. 29.   237. *Answers from the Heart*, p. 129.   238. *Our Appointment with Life*, p. 46.   239. *You Are Here*, p. 6–7.   240. *Shambhala Sun*, March 1998.

241. *Nothing to Do, Nowhere to Go*, p. 139.   242. *Answers from the Heart*, p. 16.   243. *You Are Here*, p. 16–17.   244. *Answers from the Heart*, p. 61.   245. Ibid., p. 96.   246. *Touching Peace*, p. 123.   247. Ibid., p. 121.   248. *A Rose for Your Pocket*, p. 52–53.   249. *Touching Peace*, p. 19–20.   250. *Peaceful Action, Open Heart*, p. 130.

251. *Being Peace*, p. 13.   252. *Answers from the Heart*, p. 39.   253. *Buddha Mind, Buddha Body*, p. 87.   254. *Shambhala Sun*, May 2008.   255. *Answers from the Heart*, p. 146.   256. *The Sun My Heart*, p. 39–41.   257. *Nothing to Do, Nowhere to Go*, p. 103.   258. Ibid., p. 156–57.   259. *Understanding Our Mind*, p. 245–46.   260. *You Are Here*, p. 85–88.

261. *Touching Peace*, p. 123.   262. Ibid., p. 123   263. Ibid., p. 50.   264. Ibid., p. 56.   265. *Understanding Our Mind*, p. 242–43.   266. *Calming the Fearful Mind*, p. 64–65.   267. *Shambhala Sun*, March 2006.   268. *Cultivating the Mind of Love*, p. 91–92.   269. *The Sun My Heart*, p. 17.   270. *You Are Here*, p. 15.

271. *Shambhala Sun*, July 2004.   272. Ibid., March

2006. 273. *Cultivating the Mind of Love,* p. 69–70. 274. Ibid., p. 54. 275. *Keeping the Peace,* p. 15. 276. *You Are Here,* p. 8–10. 277. Ibid., p. 5–8. 278. *Cultivating the Mind of Love,* p. 78. 279. *You Are Here,* p. 10. 280. *Answers from the Heart,* p. 95–96.

281. *Touching Peace,* p. 53. 282. *A Rose for Your Pocket,* p. 59. 283. *You Are Here,* p. 48–49. 285. *Buddha Mind, Buddha Body,* p. 49. 286. Ibid., p. 17. 287. *Transformation and Healing,* p. 34. 288. *Peaceful Action, Open Heart,* p. 128. 289. *You Are Here,* p. 42. 290. *Answers from the Heart,* p. 77.

291. *Being Peace,* p. 14. 292. *Answers from the Heart,* p. 81–82. 293. Ibid., p. 28. 294. Ibid., p. 61. 295. *Buddha Mind, Buddha Body,* p. 28. 296. *Answers from the Heart,* p. 69. 297. Ibid., p. 15. 298. *Buddha Mind, Buddha Body,* p. 26. 299. *You Are Here,* p. 11–12. 300. *Answers from the Heart,* p. 80.

301. *Buddha Mind, Buddha Body,* p. 86. 302. *Nothing to Do, Nowhere to Go,* p. 156–57. 303. Ibid., p. 155. 304. *Answers from the Heart,* p. 167–68. 305. Ibid., p. 149–50. 306. *Touching Peace,* p. 21. 307. *Nothing to Do, Nowhere to Go,* p. 155. 308. *Touching Peace,* p. 17. 309. *You Are Here,* p. 55. 310. Ibid., p. 8–9.

311. *Understanding Our Mind,* p. 245–46. 312. Ibid., p. 242–43. 313. *You Are Here,* p. 1. 314. *Being Peace,* p. 48. 315. Ibid., p. 43–46. 316. *Understanding Our Mind,* p. 245–46. 317. *Touching Peace,* p. 32. 318. *Peaceful Ac-*

tion, Open Heart, p. 244–45. 319. Answers from the Heart, p. 16. 320. Nothing to Do, Nowhere to Go, p. 11.

321. Keeping the Peace, p. 17. 322. You Are Here, p. 77. 323. Ibid., p. 55. 324. You Are Here, p. 8–10. 325. Answers from the Heart, p. 17. 326. Shambhala Sun, July 2010. 327. Answers from the Heart, p. 61–62. 328. Keeping the Peace, p. 16. 329. Touching Peace, p. 3. 330. Ibid., p. 59.

331. Shambhala Sun, July 2010. 332. Touching Peace, p. 19. 333. Answers from the Heart, p. 19. 334. Shambhala Sun, March 2006. 335. Being Peace, p. 42. 336. Answers from the Heart, p. 65. 337. Calming the Fearful Mind, p. 64–65. 338. Touching Peace, p. 17. 339. Shambhala Sun, May 2008. 340. Touching Peace, p. 57–58.

341. You Are Here, p. 13. 342. The Heart of the Buddha's Teaching, p. 121–22. 343. You Are Here, p. 107. 344. The Heart of the Buddha's Teaching, p. 132. 345. Touching Peace, p. 91. 346. Answers from the Heart, p. 122–23. 347. Touching Peace, p. 45. 348. Answers from the Heart, p. 70. 349. A Rose for Your Pocket, p. 17. 350. Love's Garden, p. xiv.

351. Touching Peace, p. 29. 352. Cultivating the Mind of Love, p. 49. 353. Touching Peace, p. 45. 354. Answers from the Heart, p. 55. 355. Reconciliation, p. 5. 356. You Are Here, p. 85–88. 357. Buddha Mind, Buddha Body, p. 1–2. 358. Touching Peace, p. 42–43. 359. Ibid., p. 90. 360. Cultivating the Mind of Love, p. 54.

361. Ibid., p. 45. 362. You Are Here, p. 5. 363. Being Peace, p. 8. 364. True Love, p. 6. 365. You Are Here, p. 118.

CREDITS

About the Author

Thich Nhat Hanh is a world-renowned Zen monk, poet, and peace activist who has been nominated for the Nobel Peace Prize. Born in Vietnam, from which he was exiled in 1966, he lives in Plum Village, a monastic community in France. He has also founded monasteries in New York, California, Mississippi, Germany, Thailand, Hong Kong, and Australia. Thich Nhat Hanh travels actively through North America, Europe, and Asia to share the art of mindful living with people of all backgrounds. He is the author of numerous books, including the best-selling *The Miracle of Mindfulness, Peace Is Every Step*, *Anger*, and *Living Buddha, Living Christ*. For more information, please visit www.plumvillage.org.

OTHER BOOKS BY THICH NHAT HANH
AVAILABLE FROM SHAMBHALA PUBLICATIONS

The Pocket Thich Nhat Hanh

The seeming simplicity of Thich Nhat Hanh's words belies the power of his teaching to touch the heart and mind and to inspire spiritual practice. These selections, taken from his many published works, together make up a concise introduction to all his major themes, and they distill his teachings on the transformation of individuals, relationships, and society.

True Love: A Practice for Awakening the Heart

We all seek the happiness that comes from loving and being loved, yet we often find ourselves dissatisfied in our relationships and unable to grasp the cause. Thich Nhat Hanh here shows the way to overcome our recurrent obstacles to love—by learning to be mindful, open, and present with ourselves and others. He also introduces the four key aspects of love described in the Buddhist tradition—loving-kindness, compassion, joy, and freedom—and describes many simple and direct ways in which we can practice authentic love in our everyday lives.

You Are Here: Discovering the Magic of the Present Moment

In our daily lives we are often lost in thought. Whether we are preoccupied with regrets about the past or fears about the future, we lose ourselves in our plans, in our anger, in our anxieties. The practice of mindfulness frees us from these obsessions, landing us firmly in the present moment—the only moment in which we can be truly alive and truly happy. In *You Are Here* the beloved Zen monk Thich Nhat Hanh offers us the insights and daily practices that will help us to experience the "miracle of mindfulness," becoming present to the wonders of being alive that are available in each and every moment of our lives.